A Teacher's Guide to United States History, Volume I

Reproducible Activities and Lesson Plans for Teaching the Age of Exploration through the Progressive Movement

Joseph C. Oswald

A Teacher's Guide to United States History, Volume I

ISBN: 0-9709734-2-X
ISBN-13: 978-0-9709734-2-9

TABLE OF CONTENTS

ABOUT THE AUTHOR

Joe Oswald currently serves as the chairman of the social studies department at Thomas Kelly High School in Chicago. He has been teaching United States history for fourteen years and holds a Bachelor of Arts degree in secondary education from De Paul University, a Master of Arts degree in history from De Paul University, and a second master's degree in educational administration from Governors State University. In addition to teaching, Joe Oswald has served on his school's Instructional Leadership Team, the AdvancED school accreditation team, the Literacy Team, coordinated the implementation of standardized test preparation and literacy improvement initiatives for the social studies department, and supervised several student teachers. He has also written a history of Chicago's historic Beverly/Morgan Park community published by Arcadia Publishing as part of their *Images of America* series and a vocabulary improvement book for students. For questions, comments, or additional information please contact Joe Oswald at joe@joeoswald.com or visit his website at joeoswald.com.

INTRODUCTION

Teaching content material while teaching important academic and life skills should be the goal of any teacher, young or old, novice or veteran. Whether a veteran teacher or new to the classroom, history teachers of all levels will find this book useful and practical with lessons that are classroom-tested and are sure to save teachers countless hours developing activities. Written by a teacher, for teachers, the lessons in this book cover the Age of Exploration through the Progressive Movement, are full of challenging yet engaging activities, and represent years of teaching diverse students of all skill levels. Teachers using this book will find reproducible lecture notes, map activities, writing assignments, cooperative learning activities, graphic organizers, quizzes, tests, and project-based lessons ready to be photocopied for use and all accompanied by lesson plans that are detailed yet adaptable. Teachers and students will find the activities in this book can be both fun and challenging yet also target important academic and literacy skills such as note-taking, outlining, reading, writing, and analyzing primary and secondary sources. Additionally, there are several projects in this book that require the use of programs such as Microsoft® PowerPoint®, Excel®, and Publisher®. These projects provide a creative and student-centered approach to teaching and learning, but these projects also teach students how to use important software programs they will be using the rest of the their academic and professional lives. Since many of these projects can have a presentation component to them, they also present a great opportunity to get students comfortable with speaking in public and enhancing their presentation skills. Though these lessons were originally designed for high school students, they can be modified for use with middle school students and the teaching of other topics in history. Finally, the activities in this book are not meant to be an all-inclusive approach to teaching United States history. They are simply suggested activities that are meant to supplement and complement what teachers are already doing in their classrooms. It is up to the individual teachers to decide how and when to use these activities and to make necessary accommodations to them based on the needs and abilities of their students.

Common Core Standards and College Readiness Standards. Standards and goals for the teaching of history vary from state to state. However, many state standards are being replaced by the new national Common Core Standards and Indicators for History and the Social Sciences as well the ACT®-created College Readiness Standards for reading. Both of these standards are literacy-based and focus on the teaching of literacy skills through the content areas, such as history. Many of the lessons in this book target various literacy skills, such as summarizing, analyzing, and evaluating texts; indentifying main ideas and supporting details; indentifying cause and effect relationships; making inferences; drawing conclusions; and vocabulary development. Activities that have a literacy focus have the corresponding Common Core Standards and College Readiness Standards listed in the accompanying lesson plan. Since United States history is taught to students in varying grades and academic levels, the skill levels referenced in this book for the these standards are somewhat subjective and can be modified to reflect the different levels of students as well as the various skills a teacher might be trying to emphasize. There is also room on the lesson plan templates for teachers to add their own state goals specific to the teaching of history.

Excel® and PowerPoint® Projects. This book contains several projects and activities that require the use of Microsoft Excel, PowerPoint, and Publisher. While these programs are widely used in schools across the country today, it should not be assumed all students know how to use these programs or are proficient with them. A certain working knowledge of these programs is required by the teacher in order to use them for classroom activities. This is especially the case with Excel since it has so many mathematical and graphing applications (which students will be required to utilize with some of the projects in this book). Therefore, teachers must be somewhat proficient with these programs and their applications so they can help students create a better final product for their assignments. For example, the Excel activities students will be asked to research and chart certain kinds of data, such as census statistics and battle casualties. The directions that accompany these activities contain examples of how to organize the necessary data in the spreadsheets, however, students will have to write the proper mathematical formulas in the proper cells to get the program to calculate and chart the data properly. This will be a learning experience for the students and a great cross-curricular activity utilizing their math skills, but the teacher should be prepared to help them with the simple mathematical equations in Excel format needed to setup the spreadsheet properly.

Furthermore, with more technological resources becoming available to students and teachers on almost a daily basis, there is no limit to the various types of engaging assignments that can be created. Designing simple websites about historical topics, engaging students in content-related blogs and online discussion forums created by the teacher, having students create Facebook biographies for historical figures, or designing geo-caching activities using GIS and GPS software are just some options available to teachers today. The more knowledgeable teachers are about these technologies the more opportunities teachers will have to connect with their students.

Notes and Study Guides. This book contains many reproducible sets of lecture notes and student study guides. It is at the teacher's discretion as to how to use these resources. The notes can be copied and given to students as handout notes, copied onto overhead projector transparencies and used as lecture notes, or retyped for use in PowerPoint presentations. Some of the notes are quite detailed, such as with the Constitution notes (the font on these notes is larger to easily facilitate the use on an overhead projector as is the case with some of the outlines. The larger the font the easier it is for students in the back of the room to read the notes). Other notes are meant to simply provide a basis for discussion or introductory background information, as with the Civil War and Industrial Revolution notes. The study guides contain several questions students should be able to answer upon completion of a chapter or unit. These questions represent what the students should have learned. It is at the teachers' discretion as to whether or not to assign the questions for homework or simply have the students use them as self-study questions. However, in either case, it is a good idea to give the students the study guide at the start of a unit since the questions and terms on the study guide represent what the students need to know. This will help guide students in their reading and studying as they progress through the unit.

LESSON PLAN
HISTORICAL TERMS AND CONCEPTS

Teacher:	Date:
Subject:	Period(s):
Title of Lesson:	State Standards:
Common Core Standards and Indicators: **RH.9-10.4.** Determine the meaning of words and phrases as they are used in a text, including vocabulary describing political, social, or economic aspects of history/social science	College Readiness Standards: **ACT-CR: Reading, ACT-CR: Score Range 13–15** **Meanings of Words:** Understand the implication of a familiar word or phrase and of simple descriptive language

Purpose/ Objective	Used as a beginning-of-the-year warm up activity, students will have a working understanding of many of the terms and concepts they will encounter throughout the year.
Materials	Assignment directions and list of terms from next page, textbook, dictionary
Procedures	Assign students the list of historical terms and concepts for them to define for homework. Give them a few days to complete the assignment then go over the definitions with them. After going over the definitions with the class, engage them in a chunking exercise on the board where they must place each term in a category…either social, political or economic. This will help them remember the terms and better understand their relationship to one another. Have students keep the definitions in their notebook so they can be referred to throughout the year.
Assessment	Collect for a notebook or homework grade. Students will take a quiz on the terms and concepts assigned to them.
Comments	

Historical Terms and Concepts

The following is a list of terms and concepts that come up throughout the study of history. It is therefore important that you have a solid understanding of these terms before we begin our studies. These terms will be referred to throughout the school year. Your first assignment is to define all the terms for homework and be prepared to be tested on them. The terms are not listed in any particular order, however, they can be grouped into social, political and economic categories. You are to keep your definitions in your notebook so you can easily refer to them in the future.

Democracy	Dictator	Agriculture/Agrarian	Diplomacy	Gold Standard
Capitalism	Tyranny	Mercantilism	Foreign Policy	Inflation
Socialism	Fascism	Totalitarianism	Domestic Policy	Monarchy
Communism	Tariff	Colonialism/Colony	Revolution	Industrialization
Nationalism	Market Economy	Imperialism	Depression	Economy
Rural	Urban	Sectionalism	Republic	Culture

Historical Terms and Concepts

The following is a list of terms and concepts that come up throughout the study of history. It is therefore important that you have a solid understanding of these terms before we begin our studies. These terms will be referred to throughout the school year. Your first assignment is to define all the terms for homework and be prepared to be tested on them. The terms are not listed in any particular order, however, they can be grouped into social, political and economic categories. You are to keep your definitions in your notebook so you can easily refer to them in the future.

Democracy	Dictator	Agriculture/Agrarian	Diplomacy	Gold Standard
Capitalism	Tyranny	Mercantilism	Foreign Policy	Inflation
Socialism	Fascism	Totalitarianism	Domestic Policy	Monarchy
Communism	Tariff	Colonialism/Colony	Revolution	Industrialization
Nationalism	Market Economy	Imperialism	Depression	Economy
Rural	Urban	Sectionalism	Republic	Culture

Age of Exploration

Background:

To the people of medieval Europe, the land known as the Americas was yet to be discovered. **Vikings**, led by **Leif Ericson**, did reach an island now called **Newfoundland** in North America off the coast of what is today Canada, in the year 1,000 A.D. The Vikings called this island Vineland because of all the vine trees. However, the Vikings were not interested in permanent settlement so they soon returned to Europe. Due to such things as religious wars (the Crusades), internal fighting, and a long battle with the Black Death (the plague), European countries were not interested in voyages of exploration until the late 15th Century (1490's). European merchants began thinking about a better way to get to the **East Indies** (**spice islands in Asia known as the Moluccas**) and **China** where precious silks and other spices were located. At the same time a new belief the world was round, not flat, began to gain in popularity. By now, Europeans had lost all knowledge of the Americas since the early Viking voyages, but the Americas were discovered again during this **Age of Exploration** when European sailors began sailing west from Europe trying to find a shorter route to Asia.

These European sailors were searching for a new **water route** to Asia, and it was **Christopher Columbus** who had the idea of sailing west from Europe to get to the East (Asia). In 1492, Columbus ("Columbus sailed the ocean blue") reached islands in the Caribbean now known as the **Bahamas**. Columbus was Italian, but he sailed for **Spain**. It was only the King and Queen of Spain who were willing to give Columbus the money and ships needed for his voyage with the promise that any riches discovered would go to Spain to help Spain pay for its costly wars. Columbus named the island he landed at **San Salvador**. He eventually made several trips to the Americas, but he died thinking he made it all the way to the East. The natives were simply called Indians. The islands where he landed came to be called the **West Indies**. Columbus never actually made it to the mainland of North America, but news of the **New World** he "discovered" reached all of Europe. Soon other explorers sailed to the New World in search of fame, riches, and for religious zeal (**God, Gold and Glory**). Many Spanish explorers soon made Spain the wealthiest and most powerful country in Europe by claiming land and its riches (gold and silver) in the New World. The contact between Europeans and the natives of the New World saw a great exchange of ideas and products (**Columbian Exchange**) that greatly affected the Old World and the New World. A mapmaker (cartographer) named the Americas after explorer, Amerigo Vespucci, who proved the Americas were newly discovered continents and NOT part of Asia.

I) European exploration starting in the late 1400s

- **A)** Reasons
  - **1)** To find another water route to Asia
    - **a)** Columbus was the first explorer to try sailing west to get to Asia
    - **b)** Landed at islands in the Caribbean
    - **c)** Thought he actually made it to the East Indies in Asia
    - **d)** Called people he found Indians
  - **2)** Later explorers were motivated by God, Gold and Glory
    - **a)** Riches
    - **b)** Land
    - **c)** Religious zeal (enthusiasm) and honor by converting Indians to Christianity

B) Countries and their Explorers

1) Spain-started to claim lands in Mexico then moved north

a) Christopher Columbus-
b) Vasco Balboa-
c) Ferdinand Magellan-
d) Francisco Coronado
e) Francisco Pizzaro-
f) Hernan Cortes- conquered Mexico

i) established Spanish empire in Mexico
ii) divided land into viceroyalties
iii) used encomiendas, haciendas, and missions to settle the region

2) France- started claiming lands in Canada then moved south

a) Explored North America looking for the Northwest Passage (shortcut to Asia)

i) Jacques Cartier-
ii) Samuel de Champlain-
iii) Marquette & Joliet-
iv) Robert de LaSalle- explored Ohio River country and Mississippi River down to Gulf of Mexico and claimed those lands for France.
He named the Louisiana region after King Louis XIV (14th) of France

b) French Empire in North America extended from Canada to Gulf of Mexico and from the Rocky Mountains to the Appalachians
c) Chains of lakes and rivers known as **water highways** connected the French Empire
d) Fur trading became the major business of French settlers
e) To encourage settlement in the New World (New France), the king granted land to wealthy upper class people **(aristocrats)**
f) Canada and Louisiana still contain French speaking populations

3) England (Britain)

a) Delay in colonization was greatly attributed to religious upheaval in England between Protestants and Catholics resulting from the Protestant Reformation
b) Very first colony was Roanoke established by Walter Raleigh in 1585 and 1587, but the colony vanished without a trace
c) English colonization increased after the defeat of the Spanish Armada in 1588 at the hands of "sea dogs" like Francis Drake and economic factors that left Spain weakened
d) Jamestown was the first successful English colony established in 1607
e) England eventually established thirteen colonies along the Atlantic Ocean and attracted the most colonists

4) Netherlands (Dutch people)-settled the East Coast areas around New York

a) also looking for another route to Asia

i) Henry Hudson landed at New York Bay (Hudson River named after him)

b) Dutch established colony on Manhattan island, which they bought from the Iroquois Indians
c) Dutch also tried to encourage settlement by granting tracks of land to wealthy people who would then turn around and rent it to settlers **(Patroon System).**
The Dutch and the French methods to encourage settlement failed. **Why?**
d) Many believe the Dutch brought the customs of Christmas to the Americas

5) Sweden-along the Delaware River.
- **a)** Small colony in 1638
- **b)** Colonists may have been first people to build log cabins in America

6) Russia-claimed land in Alaska and explored south into California
- **a)** Vitus Bering explored waters between Asia (Siberia) and Alaska-Bering Straight
- **b)** Fur trading also became important for Russia
- **c)** Russian military built outposts along the West Coast as far south as California
  - **i)** This alarmed Spanish officials, which caused them to add additional settlements and military bases in an effort to stop Russian expansion

C) African contributions to the New World

1) Africans accompanied many European explorers to the New World as servants, slaves, and free people

2) Some acted as scouts, ship builders, or soldiers
- **a)** Estevanico
  - **i)** served as a guide to Cortes and a scout for a Spanish expedition to the American Southwest
  - **ii)** heard of the Indian Seven Cities of Gold **(Cibola)**, which led to Coronado's exploration of the region in search of gold
- **b)** Jean Baptiste Point du Sable
  - **i)** Educated, Black French trader
  - **ii)** Became first person to settle in area now known as Chicago

3) As European colonies grew in America there was a shortage of labor
- **a)** Europeans tried to force Indians into slavery but many died or ran away
- **b)** African slaves were then imported as a cheap source of labor
- **c)** 10 million slaves imported from Africa over time with 400,000 eventually ending up in the English colonies

*** As more countries claimed more land territorial disputes began to heat up. Of the many results of European exploration to the Americas was the almost complete extermination of the Native American Indians from European diseases (small pox, measles, typhoid, tuberculosis, even the common cold) as well as wars of conquest; slavery; loss of lifeways (means of subsistence); and depression caused by the stripping away of Native lands, religion, and culture (suicide became very common)***

The English Colonies

After Europeans began to explore the Americas they realized the New World was very rich in raw materials and natural resources, such as gold, silver, lumber, animals and furs. They also soon realized the soil and climate in the New World was suitable for growing large numbers of crops. The Spanish claimed land in the Caribbean, South America, Mexico, the American Southwest, and Florida. The first Spanish settlement on the mainland was St. Augustine in Florida. The Spanish were the first to start bringing African slaves to the New World to work the sugar plantations in the Caribbean. France explored and claimed land from what is now Canada to the Gulf of Mexico, between the Appalachian Mountains and the Rocky Mountains, but did not settle much of that land (only about 50,000 settlers). They established a good relationship with the Indians and traded heavily with them for furs. The land between the Mississippi River and the Rocky Mountains was called Louisiana, after King Louis XIV (14th).

Working under the theory of **mercantilism**, colonies were established for benefit of the mother country. Colonies were often organized by companies (**joint-stock companies**) and granted a **charter** by the king to establish a settlement and do business in a certain area. The purpose of the colonies were to gather raw materials and natural resources and send them back to the mother country where they would be turned into finished products and sold as exports. The settlers were still citizens of the mother country and abided by its laws.

The English eventually established thirteen colonies along the Atlantic Coast from Massachusetts to Georgia (what is now Maine through Georgia. The Spanish still controlled Florida at this time) with over one million settlers by the 1750s. Most people came to the colonies as **indentured servants**. The first successful English colony was **Jamestown**, Virginia, established in 1607. These colonists were greatly helped by Powhatan Indians, particularly Pocahontas. Tobacco became the leading crop of Jamestown. Other English settlers soon followed to the New World.

The **Pilgrims**, a group of separatist Puritans, came to the New World looking for religious freedom. They settled Plymouth, Massachusetts in 1620. Before reaching land the Pilgrims drew up the **Mayflower Compact**, an agreement to establish laws and maintain order among their people. The Mayflower Compact is considered one of the first examples of a democratic form of government in the New World based on a written agreement and the consent of the governed.

Other **Puritans** (Protestants looking to "purify" the Church of England) soon came to the New World. The northern New England colonies were based on a culture of strict religious Puritan faith, a religious work ethic, and an emphasis on discipline and education. The New England colonies soon became centered on small-scale farming, fishing, ship-building, lumbering, trade, and banking. The Salem witch trials were an example of the intolerance that existed in the New England colonies.

The Middle colonies were known for slighter larger scale farming and livestock, and many colonies such as Pennsylvania were known for their religious toleration. The warmer Southern colonies revolved around large-scale farming, particularly plantation-style farming, using slave labor to produce cash crops such as tobacco, rice, indigo, sugar, and later, cotton. Slavery became entrenched in the Southern culture and economy and was eventually tied to many aspects of colonial life through the buying of goods that were products of slave labor.

LESSON PLAN
COLONIAL MAP

Teacher:	Date:
Subject:	Period(s):
Title of Lesson:	State Standards:
Common Core Standards and Indicators: **RH.11-12.7.** Integrate and evaluate multiple sources of information presented in diverse formats and media (e.g., visually, quantitatively, as well as in words) in order to address a question or solve a problem.	College Readiness Standards: **ACT-CR: Reading, ACT-CR: Score Range 16–19** **Generalizations and Conclusions:** Draw simple generalizations and conclusions about people, ideas, and so on in uncomplicated passages

Purpose/ Objective	Students will strengthen their geography and map reading skills while learning more about the English colonies. Students will understand some of the fundamental differences as to why the various colonies were founded.
Materials	Assignment directions from next page, colored pencils, textbook, blank outline map of the English colonies
Procedures	Pass out copies of the map directions contained on the following page. Allow students to work on map activity in class for a day or two and complete the rest for homework.
Assessment	This assignment can be graded by creating a rubric or simply grading it on a sliding scale. Teacher will determine the point value of the assignment. Points are subtracted for every item missing. Students can be given a quiz on the colonies as well.
Comments	Two sets of directions are contained on one page to save paper. Copy directions and cut into slips. More points should be subtracted for the more important or more time-consuming items required for the assignment.

Colonial Map Assignment

Using the blank map you were given of the English colonies and information from your textbook or other sources, you are to create your own map of the colonies with the following information.

1. Locate and label the thirteen English colonies.

2. Locate and label the following cities: Jamestown, Plymouth, Charlestown, New York, Philadelphia, Boston, Annapolis, New Bern, Williamsburg, Savannah.

3. Use three different colors on the map to distinguish the New England colonies, the Middle colonies and the Southern colonies.

4. On the map, write the name of the person or people who founded each colony, the reason it was founded, and the date it was founded.

5. Create a map key.

Colonial Map Assignment

Using the blank map you were given of the English colonies and information from your textbook or other sources, you are to create your own map of the colonies with the following information.

1. Locate and label the thirteen English colonies.

2. Locate and label the following cities: Jamestown, Plymouth, Charlestown, New York, Philadelphia, Boston, Annapolis, New Bern, Williamsburg, Savannah.

3. Use three different colors on the map to distinguish the New England colonies, the Middle colonies and the Southern colonies.

4. On the map, write the name of the person or people who founded each colony, the reason it was founded, and the date it was founded.

5. Create a map key.

Name______________________________

U.S. History Quiz
Colonization of the New World

1. Why did Columbus sail west from Europe and where was he going?
2. What European country gave Columbus the money and ships for his voyage?
3. What was the first major European country to claim land in the New World?
4. What person defeated the Aztecs to take control of Mexico?
5. List the three major reasons that motivated explorers to come to the New World?
6. Where did France claim land in the New World?
7. Where was the first successful English settlement?
8. What are crops called that are grown specifically to be sold for profit?
9. Most people came to the English colonies as what (their status)?
10. How many colonies did the English eventually establish in America?
11. Which European country had the best relationship with the various Indians?
12. What eventually became the main source of cheap labor in the southern colonies?
13. Explain the economic differences between the northern and southern colonies.
14. Define the economic theory of mercantilism.
15. What main Christian religious faith were the Pilgrims and other Puritans?

The French and Indian War

By the 1750s the French and English settlers in North America started to come into contact with each other in the Ohio River Valley. A struggle for land soon developed and turned into a full-scale war between France and England. In North America it was called the French and Indian War.

The **French and Indian War** lasted from 1754 to 1763 and coincided with the Seven Years War being fought in Europe between England and France over their world-wide struggle for land and empires. The French had established a good relationship with the Indians, particularly over the fur trade. The relationship between the Indians and the English was not as good because the English were viewed mostly as wanting to take Indian land. Thus, the French had the support of many Indians.

Once the war broke out France and Britain sent large military forces to America where they were to fight the war with the help of their own colonists. At a meeting in Albany, New York among colonial representatives to discuss a plan for defense, Benjamin Franklin, a wealthy and influential English colonists from Pennsylvania, suggested the **Albany Plan of Union**. This was an effort to unite the colonies under a common goal and common leadership. It was rejected by colonial governments and by the English **Parliament** due to fear of losing control over the colonies and because Parliament believed the colonies could not work together. The Albany Plan of Union was important because it is considered the first attempt to unite the colonies and because England underestimated the colonies' ability to cooperate.

England won the war, which officially ended in 1763 with the **Treaty of Paris**. France was forced to give up its land in North America, including Canada and all land east of the Mississippi River, to Britain. Spain helped France in this conflict and in anticipation of a loss, France awarded New Orleans and the rest of the Louisiana Territory to Spain in 1762 (in a secret treaty Napoleon Bonaparte of France regained control of Louisiana from Spain in 1800, officially transferred in 1803).

The French and Indian War cost England a great deal of money, which England looked to the colonies to help pay for through increased taxes. To avoid future conflicts in North America, England also decided to maintain a standing army in the colonies. England thought both measures were justified since the colonists benefited from the victory and increased military presence. However, many of the colonists deeply resented the new taxes, claiming many of them were unfair and "**taxation without representation**."

Many of the colonists also viewed some of the new laws and standing army as a violation of their rights as English citizens. These differences would eventually escalate to a call for independence from England and a war to win that independence. The Declaration of Independence established the United States of America out of the thirteen original English colonies and their victory over England in the American Revolution secured the United States as an officially recognized, independent, and **sovereign** country.

LESSON PLAN
WORKING WITH A FORMAL OUTLINE

Teacher:	Date:
Subject:	Period(s):
Title of Lesson:	State Standards:
Common Core Standards and Indicators: **RH.11-12.2.** Determine the central ideas or information of a primary or secondary source; provide an accurate summary that makes clear the relationships among the key details and ideas	College Readiness Standards: **ACT-CR: Reading, ACT-CR: Score Range 16–19** **Main Ideas and Author's Approach:** Identify a clear main idea or purpose of straightforward paragraphs in uncomplicated literary narratives; **Supporting Details:** Locate simple details at the sentence and paragraph level in uncomplicated passages

Purpose/ Objective	To teach students the fundamentals of working with a formal outline that can be used when taking notes, collecting and organizing information, or preparing for a writing assignment. This activity is also meant to improve students' reading and organizational skills as well as provide a foundation for the initial steps of writing.
Materials	Copies of formal outline example and sample outline on the events leading to the American Revolution from the following pages, transparencies of the outline
Procedures	Pass out copies of formal outline example and sample outline to students. Put transparency of the formal outline on the overhead projector and ask students to follow along as the structure of the outline is explained. Do the same with the sample outline related to the American Revolution. Teach students how a textbook uses headings and sub-headings to organize information. Teach students to use capital letters in the outline to form main ideas. Teach students to use the information in the paragraphs to fill in other relevant information and supporting details.
Assessment	Students can be instructed to read pages in their textbook and take notes using the formal outline structure. Students can then be assigned a notebook grade. Points should not be taken off until students understand this process.
Comments	Formal outlines can be effective because they force students to digest information more so than when simply asked to answer questions because students have to do more than simply hunt for key words or copy sentences. This skill will take time and patience and should be reinforced throughout the year. The book used for this example is *American Nation* by Paul Boyer, published by Holt, Rinehart and Winston; copyright 2007

Formal Outline Framework

I Topic

A) Main Idea

1. Supporting Details
    a. additional details
2. Supporting Details
3. Supporting Details
    a. additional details
        i. additional details
    b. additional details
    c. additional details
        i. additional details
        ii. additional details

B) Main Idea

1. Supporting Details
2. Supporting Details
3. Supporting Details

C) Main Idea

1. Supporting Details
2. Supporting Details
3. Supporting Details

D) Main Idea

1. Supporting Details
2. Supporting Details
3. Supporting Details

Sample Formal Outline

Tips: Look for topic sentences in each paragraph to help indentify main ideas.
Preview terms and questions in section review to know what will be important.
Include all bold-faced words in text and terms listed in the section review.

I) The Seeds of Unrest

A) Governing New Territories
1. American Indians grew upset over the large number of settlers on their land
2. In Pontiac's Rebellion Indians tried to push settlers off their land
3. As a result, England (Britain) passed the Proclamation of 1763
   a. This prohibited colonists from settling west of the Appalachian Mountains to avoid future conflicts with Indians
   b. This was impossible to enforce and colonists resented having their freedom to settle lands they fought for restricted

B) Financing the Empire
1. England was in debt after the French and Indian War and looked to raise money by taxing the colonies
2. The Sugar Act of 1764 imposed a duty (import tax) on sugar items
   a. The Sugar Act hurt colonial business related to sugar items
   b. Colonial merchants formed committees to protest the law
3. The Stamp Act of 1765 placed a tax on printed matter such as legal documents, newspapers, diplomas, and playing cards

C) Colonial Protest
1. Colonists were upset and claimed Stamp Act was unfair and was "taxation without representation" because the colonies were not represented in Parliament
2. Colonists signed non-importation agreements (boycotts) for British goods to protest the Stamp Act
3. The Sons of Liberty was formed to protest British actions
   a. Lawyers, merchants, artisans and politicians
      i. Sam Adams was a founder of the Boston Sons of Liberty
4. Stamp Act Congress was formed to officially protest Stamp Act to King and Parliament
5. Stamp Act was repealed in 1766

D) Declaratory Act of 1766
1. Asserted Parliament's right to tax the colonies

E) Townshend Acts

LESSON PLAN
ROAD TO INDEPENDENCE
FILL-IN-THE-BLANK NOTES

Teacher:		Date:
Subject:		Period(s):
Title of Lesson:		State Standards:
Common Core Standards and Indicators:		College Readiness Standards:
Purpose/ Objective	Students will understand the background and major events that led the English colonists to seek independence from their mother country.	
Materials	Copies of the blank fill-in-the-blank notes from the following pages, transparencies of the fill-in-the-blank notes with the answers from the following pages	
Procedures	Teacher will pass out copies of blank fill-in-the-blank lecture notes on the American Revolution. Teacher will put the transparencies of the fill-in-the-blank notes on the overhead projector and use to guide students through lecture notes on the events leading up to the American Revolution. Students should follow along and write the missing information in the blanks on their outline notes.	
Assessment	Students will be quizzed and tested on this information. These notes can also serve as the basis of information for other activities such as the graphic organizer on events leading to the American Revolution and the American Revolution PowerPoint project.	
Comments	There our several pages of notes contained in this outline. Teacher should not spend the entire class period lecturing. These notes take a few days to go through and class time should be alternated between taking notes and other activities.	

Road to Independence

1. Colonial Involvement in French and British Disputes

The colonists had previously taken part in three ______________________ France and Britain had fought over ______________________ in America. In the______________________ the French pushed south of their ______________________ region into the ______________________, which the British claimed was their territory. Virginia's governor sent 21-year-old ______________________ (a member of Virginia's militia) to warn off the French. The French said they were not leaving except by ______________________. The first shots of the ______________________ were fired in 1754. At a ______________________ meeting to discuss protection from the French, ____________________ suggested a ______________________ council with a president general to organize the war effort. This plan was the ______________________ . Although it was rejected by all the colonial assemblies, it was the first step to ______________________ all the colonies.

Because the plan failed the king of England didn't take unity seriously in the future.

2. The French and Indian War

William Pitt became Britain's Prime Minister in 1756. He supplied the colonies with _________ and ______________________, and soon the war turned in England's favor. ______________________ colonists fought in the war for England. ______________________ finally won the war in 1763. The ______________________ officially ended the war and stated the terms of __________________. England gained much land but now also had a large ______________________, navy, and _________ that had to be paid off. England thought the ______________________ should help pay for the war (through taxation) since the colonies ______________________ from England's victory. Unlike the other ______________________, Britain kept troops in the colonies after the French and Indian War.

3. Proclamation of 1763

To control problems between settlers and Indians, King George III issued a proclamation, which ______________________ settlers from entering lands west of Appalachian Mountains. It also said only licensed ______________________ representing the king could trade with the ______________________. These actions ______________________ the colonists because they thought only ______________________ would benefit from the lands won from France. Colonists also thought they were not being allowed to move west because it would be harder for the ______________________ to control them.

4. British Attitudes Towards Colonies Change After 1763

The British ______________________ towards colonies before 1763 was more hands off and supported more colonial self-government. The King would request money or new laws and the colonies would say "yes" or "no." This was known as the ______________________ Requisition system. After 1763, Britain wanted to control, __________________, and __________________ the colonies more.

WHY?

Britain thought there was not going to be any more wars in America and would then not need the colonists' cooperation as much. Also, the Enlightenment movement in 18th century Europe called for more government control by some writers and those ideas were adopted in Britain.

5. More British Control and Taxation

In 1763, George Grenville became Prime Minister in Britain, and in ____________________ he issued his ____________________ to give Britain more control over the ____________________ and make the colonies ____________________ a share of the British war debt. He ordered stricter control of the ____________________ (passed in 1651), which said certain colonial products could only be shipped to England or other ____________________. These products, or ____________________, were usually raw materials such as lumber, tobacco, and cotton. This was to control colonial ____________________ and limit industrialization (production of finished products) in the colonies. Britain also regulated the sale and manufacturing of certain finished products.

WHY?

Mercantilism... Britain wanted the colonies to supply England with raw materials and also be dependent on England for finished products.

A) Currency Act (1764)

The Currency Act prohibited individual colonies from ______________________________.

B) Sugar Act (1764)

This act imposed a ____________________ (tax on imported/exported goods) on sugar, wine, cloth, and coffee from areas not belonging to ____________________. The tariff on sugar from other British colonies made the ____________________ a real tax, and it hurt the ____________ of colonial merchants who relied on sugar from the ____________ to make rum.

C) Quartering Act (1765)

The colonists wondered why troops were still in the colonies when they were no longer needed. Colonists resented this, and the colonists began to think the ______________________ were not there to protect them but to enforce British ______________________.

D) Stamp Act (1765)

The Stamp Act said certain printed items and legal ______________________ must have an ______________________ on them. The Stamp Act was the first ________________tax imposed on the colonists, and it affected nearly everyone in the colonies. For these reasons American colonists resisted the ________________ and began to claim the tax was __________________________.

6. Bases of Colonial Resistance

Resistance against a king dated back to ______________________ when King John tried to change the ______________________ of England without the ______________________ of his Great Council (wealthy landowners that represented the people of England). The ______________________ rebelled and forced King John to sign the ______________, setting the precedent for subjects having the right of ___________________. This notion of resistance carried through to the American colonies.

7. Colonial Resistance

______________________ of the Virginia ______________________ was one of the first people to speak out against British ______________________ (harsh and unfair government) in 1765. In 1775, he would speak his famous words " ____." In 1765, ______________________ organized the ______________________ in Boston. This society of lawyers, _______________________, and artisans _______________________ (refuse to buy) British _______________________. Since the _______________________ were not _______________________ in British Parliament (England's law-making body), many colonists felt the Stamp Act was "_______________________" and therefore illegal. Leaders of nine colonies met in _________________ to discuss the problem. This _______________________ decided to ask Britain to repeal the Stamp Act. In 1766, Britain's Parliament _______________________ the _______________________ under pressure from British _______________________ who were losing money from the American _______________________. Some colonial legislatures also _______________________ the _______________________ and refused to support British troops.

8. Other British Measures

The same day the _______________________ was repealed, the _______________________ was passed, which said the King and Parliament had the right to _______________________ and pass ____________ for the colonies in all cases. This was a complete turn from the _________________ system, and it also refuted the complaint that _______________________ was illegal. Between 1767 - 1770, Charles Townshend (Chancellor of the Exchequer) got _______________________ to pass the _______________________, which placed taxes on many goods bought by the colonists (glass, lead, paint, tea). He also ordered any colonial legislature that opposed the _______________________ be suspended (not allowed to meet). Vice-Admiralty Courts were also instated. This law stated that if anyone was caught trying to avoid the _______________________ they would be tried by a British naval court and not by a ________________ of their peers (which was also granted in the Magna Carta). Colonists resented these measures even more because they felt they might end all colonial self-government. More colonial ___________________ took place followed by leaders agreeing to more non-importation agreements for British goods. More British officials were sent to ____________ taxes and search for smugglers. The years 1767-1770 were years of turmoil for the colonists as some spoke out against British ____________________, and others still considered themselves loyal ________ of the king. By 1770, the ____________________ were also repealed (except for the tea tax), and all colonial legislatures were allowed to meet again.

9. Tensions Rise

(A) Boston Massacre (March 5, 1770)

A crowd of ____________________ gathered in front of Customs House and started harassing ______________. A shot was fired by someone, then other soldiers opened fire. Five men were killed, including the first to die, _________________ (a former slave). _______________ engraved prints of the event spread throughout Boston and caused many colonists to hate the British.

B) Committees of Correspondence

Committees were established by ___________________, who tried to keep colonists informed about various British actions. Some tried to convince people that a break with _______________ was necessary to preserve their liberty.

C) Tea Act

This law excused the _________________________ from paying the tax on tea because it was going bankrupt, and in effect, made it sole the provider of tea for the colonies (_________________). The company used their own agents rather than colonial merchants, hurting colonial business. It lowered the price of ___________ thinking no one would notice the tea _______________. The Tea Act and the monopolistic actions of the company, plus the loss of merchant, ____________________led to much resentment among the colonists. This in turn led to the ______________________ (December 1773) where thousands of pounds of tea were dumped into Boston harbor by the Sons of Liberty who disguised themselves as Mohawk Indians. This event led ____________________ to pass the Coercive Acts (Intolerable Acts).

D) Intolerable (Coercive) Acts

The Intolerable Acts (called this by people who couldn't take it anymore) consisted of _______ laws.

1) *Boston Port Bill (only for Massachusetts):*

- closed Boston harbor until someone admitted and paid for Tea Party

-____

2) *Massachusetts Government Act (only for Massachusetts):*

-____

-____

- king would now appoint governor and council. General Gage was appointed military governor of Massachusetts.

3. *Administration and Justice Act (only for Massachusetts):*

- permitted for change of venue (to be tried for a crime elsewhere) for British officials. WHY?

4. *New Quartering Act (all colonies)*:

-____

E). Quebec Act (1774)

This law gave the Ohio Valley (OH, IN, IL, MI, WI) to the citizens of Quebec, Canada. It allowed French people to ____________________ their ____________________ in a new region. This act was intended to buy loyalty from the French people under British rule, and it angered the colonists because ____________________ they fought for in the ____________________ was now given back to the French. It also angered colonists because French ____________________ were allowed into the area. This scared ____________________ because the French legal system did NOT have ________________, a cornerstone of the English legal system the English colonists enjoyed.

10. First Continental Congress (Philadelphia, September 1774)

Delegates from the colonies met in Philadelphia to discuss grievances against _______________. All colonies except ______________ sent delegates. They agreed on the ____________________, which said the Intolerable Acts were ____________________ and told people to disobey them. It also called on the militia to stockpile _________________ and __________________. The ______________________________ was also issued. This document was sent to the king stating the position of the colonists. The delegates disagreed on the ______________________, which was an idea for a joint parliament and a way to be taxed with representation. The _________________ was organized and provided for the first written agreement pledging colonies to work ___________. A third attempt to ______________ British goods failed because Britain did not back down this time. Congress provided for a _________________________ the following year if matters did not improve.

11. Military Preparations

Colonial militias began to drill openly in Massachusetts and other ____________________. Special ____________________ of men were organized who could be ready to fight immediately (minutemen).

12. War Begins

General ____________________ was given orders to put down all signs of ____________________. On ____________________, 750 British soldiers left Boston for ____________________ where colonial military ______________ were stored. The British were watched by ______________, who, in his famous ____________________, road ahead to warn the colonists about the British and to turn out their militia. On April 19, 1775, the British soldiers met the Massachusetts' militia at ___________ and killed eight men, then marched on to ________________. The British ________________ destroyed the military supplies at _______________ but were attacked on the way back to ___________. The first shot of the Revolutionary War was fired at Lexington, Massachusetts on April 19, 1775 and was later known as the__________________________.

Road to Independence

1. Colonial Involvement in French and British Disputes

The colonists had previously taken part in three ____**wars**____ France and Britain had fought over ____**land**____ in America. In ____**1754**____ the French pushed south of their ____**Great Lakes**____ region into the ____**Ohio River Valley**, which the British also claimed was their territory. Virginia's governor sent 21-year old **George Washington** (a member of Virginia's militia) to warn off the French. The French said they were not leaving except by ____**force**____. The first shots of the ____**French and Indian War**____ were fired in 1754. At a ____**colonial**____ meeting to discuss protection from the French, **Benjamin Franklin** suggested a ____**representative**____ council with a president general to organize the war effort. This plan was the ____**Albany Plan of Union**____. Although it was rejected by all the colonial assemblies, it was the first step to ____**uniting**____ all the colonies.

Because the plan failed the king of England didn't take unity seriously in the future.

2. The French and Indian War

William Pitt became Britain's Prime Minister in 1756. He supplied the colonies with ____**men**____ and ____**money**____, and soon the war turned in England's favor.____**25,000**____ colonists fought in the war for England. ____**England**____ finally won the war in 1763. The ____**Treaty of Paris of 1763**____ officially ended the war and stated the terms of ____**France's defeat**. England gained much land but now also had a large ____**army**____, navy, and ____**war debt**____ that had to be paid off. England thought the ____**colonies**____ should help pay for the war (through taxation) since the colonies ______**benefited**______ from England's victory. Unlike the other ______**wars**______, Britain kept troops in the colonies after the French and Indian War.

3. Proclamation of 1763

To control problems between settlers and Indians, King George III issued a proclamation, which ______**prohibited**______ settlers from entering lands west of Appalachian Mountains. It also said only licensed ______**merchants**______ representing the king could trade with the ______**Indians**______. These actions ______**angered**______ the colonists because they thought only ______**Britain**______ would benefit from the lands won from France. Colonists also thought they were not being allowed to move west because it would be harder for the ______**British**______ to control them.

4. British Attitudes Towards Colonies Change After 1763

The British ______**policy**______ towards colonies before 1763 was more hands off and supported more colonial self-government. The King would request money or new laws and the colonies would say "yes" or "no." This was known as the ______**Royal**______ Requisition system. After 1763, Britain wanted to control, ______**tax**______, and ______**regulate**______ the colonies more.

WHY?

Britain thought there was not going to be any more wars in America and would then not need the colonists' cooperation as much. Also, the Enlightenment movement in 18th century Europe called for more government control by some writers and those ideas were adopted in Britain.

5. More British Control and Taxation

In 1763, George Grenville became Prime Minister in Britain, and in ___**1764**___ he issued his ___**policies**___ to give Britain more control over the ___**colonies**___ and make the colonies ___**pay**___ a share of the British war debt. He ordered stricter control of the ___**Navigation Acts**___ (passed in 1651), which said certain colonial products could only be shipped to England or other ___**British colonies**___. These products, or ___**enumerated articles**___, were usually raw materials such as lumber, tobacco, and cotton. This was to control colonial ___**trade**___ and limit industrialization (production of finished products) in the colonies. Britain also regulated the sale and manufacturing of certain finished products.

WHY?

Mercantilism... Britain wanted the colonies to supply England with raw materials and also be dependent on England for finished products.

A) Currency Act (1764)

The Currency Act prohibited individual colonies from ___**printing their own paper money**___.

B) Sugar Act (1764)

This act imposed a ___**tariff**___ (tax on imported/exported goods) on sugar, wine, cloth, and coffee from areas not belonging to ___**the British Empire**___. The tariff on sugar from other British colonies made the ___**Sugar Act**___ a real tax, and it hurt the ___**profits**___ of colonial merchants who relied on sugar from the ___**West Indies**___ to make rum.

C) Quartering Act (1765)

The colonists wondered why troops were still in the colonies when they were no longer needed. Colonists resented this, and the colonists began to think the ____**British soldiers**________ were not there to protect them but to enforce British ________**laws**________.

D) Stamp Act (1765)

The Stamp Act said certain printed items and legal ________**documents**________ must have an ____**official seal or stamp**____ on them. The Stamp Act was the first ____**direct**______ tax imposed on the colonists, and it affected nearly everyone in the colonies. For these reasons American colonists resisted the __**Stamp Act**_ and began to claim the tax was "__**Taxation without representation."**

6. Bases of Colonial Resistance

Resistance against a king dated back to ________**1215**__________ when King John tried to change the ________**laws**________ of England without the ________**consent**________ of his Great Council (wealthy landowners that represented the people of England). The __**Great Council**___ rebelled and forced King John to sign the ____**Magna Carta**_____, setting the precedent for subjects having the right of ______**resistance**______. This notion of resistance carried through to the American colonies.

7. Colonial Resistance

________**Patrick Henry**______ of the Virginia ______**House of Burgesses**_______ was one of the first people to speak out against British ______**tyranny**______ (harsh and unfair government) in 1765. In 1775, he would speak his famous words " ______**Give me liberty or give me death**________." In 1765, ___**Samuel Adams**___ organized the ______**Sons of Liberty**______ in Boston. This society of lawyers, **merchants**, and artisans **boycotted** (refuse to buy) British **goods**. Since the **American colonies** were not **represented** in British Parliament (England's law-making body), many colonists felt the Stamp Act was " **taxation without representation** " and therefore illegal. Leaders of nine colonies met in **New York** to discuss the problem. This **Stamp Act Congress** decided to ask Britain to repeal the Stamp Act. In 1766, Britain's Parliament **repealed** the **Stamp Act** under pressure from British **merchants** who were losing money from the American **boycott**. Some colonial legislatures also **protested** the **Quartering Act** and refused to support British troops.

8. Other British Measures

The same day the **Stamp Act** was repealed, the **Declaratory Act** was passed, which said the King and Parliament had the right to **tax** and pass **laws** for the colonies in all cases. This was a complete turn from the **Royal Requisition** system, and it also refuted the complaint that **taxation without representation** was illegal. Between 1767 - 1770, Charles Townshend (Chancellor of the Exchequer) got **Parliament** to pass the **Townshend Duties**, which placed taxes on many goods bought by the colonists (glass, lead, paint, tea). He also ordered any colonial legislature that opposed the **Quartering Act** be suspended (not allowed to meet). Vice-Admiralty Courts were also instated. This law stated that if anyone was caught trying to avoid the **taxes** they would be tried by a British naval court and not by a **jury** of their peers (which was also granted in the Magna Carta). Colonists resented these measures even more because they felt they might end all colonial self-government. More colonial **boycotts** took place followed by leaders agreeing to more non-importation agreements for British goods. More British officials were sent to ____**collect**__ taxes and search for smugglers. The years 1767-1770 were years of turmoil for the colonists as some spoke out against British ________**policies**______, and others still considered themselves loyal ___**subjects**___ of the king. By 1770, the ____**Townshend Duties**__ were also repealed (except for the tea tax), and all colonial legislatures were allowed to meet again.

9. Tensions Rise

(A) Boston Massacre (March 5, 1770)

A crowd of ________**protestors**_______ gathered in front of Customs House and started harassing ___**British soldiers**___. A shot was fired by someone, then other soldiers opened fire. Five men were killed, including the first to die, ________**Crispus Attucks**____ (a former slave). __**Paul Revere's**__ engraved prints of the event spread throughout Boston and caused many colonists to hate the British.

B) Committees of Correspondence

Committees were established by ________**Sam Adams**_________, who tried to keep colonists informed about various British actions. Some tried to convince people that a break with ______**Britain**_____ was necessary to preserve their liberty.

C) Tea Act

This law excused the ___**British East India Company**___ from paying the tax on tea because it was going bankrupt, and in effect, made it the sole provider of tea for the colonies (_**creating a monopoly**_). The company used their own agents rather than colonial merchants, hurting colonial business. It lowered the price of ____**tea**________ thinking no one would notice the tea _____**tax**______. The Tea Act and the monopolistic actions of the company, plus the loss of merchant ______**business**________, led to much resentment among the colonists. This in turn led to the **Boston Tea Party** (December 1773) where thousands of pounds of tea were dumped into Boston harbor by the Sons of Liberty who disguised themselves as Mohawk Indians. This event led **Britain** to pass the Coercive Acts (Intolerable Acts).

D) Intolerable (Coercive) Acts

The Intolerable Acts (called this by people who couldn't take it anymore) consisted of **four** laws.

1) *Boston Port Bill (only for Massachusetts):*

- closed Boston harbor until someone admitted and paid for Tea Party
- **caused financial stress for colonial merchants**

2) *Massachusetts Government Act (only for Massachusetts.):*

- **disrupted government in Massachusetts**
- **reduced the number of town meetings to one per year**
- king would now appoint governor and council. General Gage was appointed military governor of Massachusetts.

3. *Administration and Justice Act (only for Massachusetts):*

- permitted for change of venue (to be tried for a crime elsewhere) for British officials. WHY?

4. *New Quartering Act (all colonies):*

- **called for British troops to be housed in private buildings and homes**

E). Quebec Act (1774)

This law gave the Ohio Valley (OH, IN, IL, MI, WI) to the citizens of Quebec, Canada. It allowed French people to ______**retain**______ their ______**customs**______ in a new region. This act was intended to buy loyalty from the French people under British rule, and it angered the colonists because ______**land**______ they fought for in the ______**French and Indian War**______ was now given back to the French. It also angered colonists because French ______**Catholics**______ were allowed into the area. This scared ______**the English colonists**______ because the French legal system did NOT have ______**trial by jury**______, a cornerstone of the English legal system the English colonists enjoyed.

10. First Continental Congress (Philadelphia, September 1774)

Delegates from the colonies met in Philadelphia to discuss grievances against ______**Britain**______. All colonies except ______**Georgia**______ sent delegates. They agreed on the ______**Suffolk Resolves**______, which said the Intolerable Acts were ______**illegal**______ and told people to disobey them. It also called on the militia to stockpile ______**weapons**______ and ______**ammunition**______. The ______**Declaration of Rights and Grievances**______ was also issued. This document was sent to the king stating the position of the colonists. The delegates disagreed on the ______**Galloway Plan**______, which was an idea for a joint parliament and a way to be taxed with representation. The ______**Continental Association**______ was organized and provided for the first written agreement pledging colonies to work ______**together**______. A third attempt to ______**boycott**______ British goods failed because Britain did not back down this time. Congress provided for a ______**Second Continental Congress**______ the following year if matters did not improve.

11. Military Preparations

Colonial militias began to drill openly in Massachusetts and other ___**colonies**___. Special ______**units**______ of men were organized who could be ready to fight immediately (minutemen).

12. War Begins

General ____**Gage**________ was given orders to put down all signs of ____**rebellion**________. On __**April 18, 1775**__________, 750 British soldiers left Boston for __**Concord, Massachusetts**__ where colonial military ______**supplies**______ were stored. The British were watched by **Paul Revere**, who, in his famous "__**midnight ride**____," road ahead to warn the colonists about the British and to turn out their militia. On April 19, 1775, the British soldiers met the Massachusetts' militia at __**Lexington**__ and killed eight men, then marched on to ______**Concord**_____. The British ______**Redcoats**______ destroyed the military supplies at ______**Concord**________ but were attacked on the way back to _____**Boston**___. The first shot of the Revolutionary War was fired at Lexington, Massachusetts on April 19, 1775 and was later known as the **"shot heard around the world."**

LESSON PLAN
GRAPHIC ORGANIZER
EVENTS LEADING TO THE AMERICAN REVOLUTION

Teacher:	Date:
Subject:	Period(s):
Title of Lesson:	State Standards:
Common Core Standards and Indicators: **RH.11-12.2.** Determine the central ideas or information of a primary or secondary source; provide an accurate summary that makes clear the relationships among the key details and ideas	College Readiness Standards: **ACT-CR: Reading, ACT-CR: Score Range 16–19 Generalizations and Conclusions:** Draw simple generalizations and conclusions about people, ideas, and so on in uncomplicated passages **; Score Range 20–23, Sequential, Comparative, and Cause-Effect Relationships** Identify clear relationships between people, ideas, and so on in uncomplicated passages

Purpose/ Objective	Students will gain a better understanding of the events that led to the American Revolution while enhancing their reading, writing, summarization, and critical thinking skills.
Materials	Copies of blank graphic organizer contained on following pages, transparency of graphic organizer completed with possible answers contained on following pages, textbook or other sources such as the Internet
Procedures	Teacher will distribute blank copies of graphic organizer to students and explain the assignment. Students are to use their textbook or other sources and write a summary of each event listed and indentify the importance or effect of each event listed. When assignment is completed teacher should display the transparency of the completed graphic organizer on the overhead projector and go over possible answers with the students so they can check their work.
Assessment	Assignment can be graded on a standard scale with points taken off for each item missed or a rubric can be designed. Students will be quizzed and tested on this information. These notes can also serve as information for other activities, such as American Revolution PowerPoint project.
Comments	Teacher can collect and grade the assignment before going over the answers or give the students a chance to correct their work by going over the answers with the students before the assignment is collected. This is always at the teacher's discretion and depends on the level of the students and difficulty of assignment. The completed graphic organizer can also be used simply as handout notes or as lecture notes.

Events Leading to the American Revolution

Name____________________________

Event	**Date**	**Summary of Event**	**Importance or Effect**
French and Indian War	1754-1763		
Proclamation of 1763	1763		
Sugar Act	1764		
Stamp Act	1765		
Sons of Liberty	1765		
Quartering Act	1765		

Event	**Date**	**Summary of Event**	**Importance or Effect**
Declaratory Act	1766		
Townshend Acts	1767		
Boston Massacre	1770		
Governor and judges of Massachusetts to be paid by King George III	1772		
Tea Act	1773		
Coercive/Intolerable Acts	1774		

Event	**Date**	**Summary of Event**	**Importance or Effect**
Quebec Act	1774		
First Continental Congress	1774		
Paul Revere's Ride	1775		
Lexington and Concord	1775		
Second Continental Congress	1775		
Olive Branch Petition	1775		

Events Leading to the American Revolution

Name________________________

Event	Date	Summary of Event	Importance or Effect
French and Indian War	1754-1763	A struggle for land between the French and British broke out in the Ohio River Valley leading to a major war. The Indians first sided with the French. The Albany Plan of Union was proposed.	France ceded Canada and all land up to the Mississippi River to Britain. To pay for the war Britain started to tax and regulate the colonies more. This eventually led to the American Revolution.
Proclamation of 1763	1763	Britain passed this law prohibiting settlement west of the Appalachian Mountains by the colonists to prevent any future conflicts and required fur traders to obtain royal permission before entering the territory.	Colonists resented having their freedoms restricted and resented having fought in a war to win this land they now could not use. However, this law was hard to enforce, and settlers and traders continued to move into the territory anyway.
Sugar Act	1764	Parliament placed a duty (import tax) on foreign sugar, molasses, and other items coming into the colonies to raise revenue. Royal inspectors began to search for smuggled goods to enforce the law.	Merchants resented this new tax and formed committees to protest the law. Colonists also refused to cooperate with British officials.
Stamp Act	1765	This wide-reaching law imposed a tax in the form of a stamp or official seal that had to be placed on various types of printed materials such as newspapers, diplomas, legal documents, and even playing cards.	Colonists were outraged and claimed tax was "taxation without representation." They signed non-importation agreements, targeted tax agents, formed the Sons of Liberty, and organized the Stamp Act Congress.
Sons of Liberty	1765	Secret committees of artisans, lawyers, merchants, and others who opposed the Stamp Act and other British measures. Sam Adams was the leader of the Boston Sons of Liberty.	Became instrumental in protesting and informing people about British actions and aggressions.
Quartering Act	1765	Law that required colonists to provide room and board for British soldiers stationed in the colonies after the French and Indian War.	Colonists resented their money being used to pay for soldiers. Viewed law as a threat to their liberties and came to view soldiers as a threat their freedoms.

Event	**Date**	**Summary of Event**	**Importance or Effect**
Declaratory Act	1766	Parliament repealed the Stamp Act but passed the Declaratory Act asserting Parliament's power to still make laws and taxes.	This act did nothing to settle the dispute over whether or not the colonies could be taxed since they had no official representation in Parliament.
Townshend Acts	1767	Laws that placed taxes on such common items as glass, tea, lead, and paint. British officials used search warrants called writs of assistance to search for smuggled goods.	Colonial courts often refused to issue writs of assistance to British officials. King stationed even more troops in the colonies because of the colonial opposition. Colonists refused to drink tea and made their own cloth.
Boston Massacre	1770	A group of British soldiers fired into an unarmed group of colonial protesters who had gathered outside the Boston custom's house to protest taxes and were harassing the soldiers. Five colonists were killed.	Colonists were outraged and began to fear and resent the British soldiers even more. Colonist believed their rights of Englishmen continued to be under attack. Paul Revere made his famous engraving of the event. John Adams defended the soldiers to make sure they got a fair trial. The soldiers were branded.
Governor and judges of Massachusetts to be paid by King George III	1772	King put governor and judges on his payroll rather than allowing them to continue being paid by the colonial legislature.	Colonists feared the governor and judges would no longer carry out their duties fairly. Sam Adams and other colonists formed Committees of Correspondence to keep people informed about British actions.
Tea Act	1773	In order to help the struggling British East India Company, Parliament passed this act that excused the company from paying certain duties and allowed them to sell tea directly to American agents.	Colonists feared this would give the East India Company a monopoly on tea sales and thereby hurt colonial merchants. The Sons of Liberty disguised themselves as Indians and destroyed a shipment of tea in Boston Harbor (Boston Tea Party).
Coercive/Intolerable Acts	1774	Parliament passed a series of laws designed to punish Massachusetts for the Tea Party. Port of Boston was closed	Other colonies sympathized with Massachusetts and began to realize the attack on Massachusetts' liberties was an attack on all of the colonies. Other colonies sent supplies.

Event	Date	Summary of Event	Importance or Effect
Quebec Act	1774	This British law extended Quebec's boundaries to the Ohio River negating the claims of other colonies to this land. It also granted religious freedom to French Catholics.	Colonists began to unite even more against what they viewed as British oppression and tyranny.
First Continental Congress	1774	All colonies except Georgia sent delegates to Philadelphia to discuss their grievances with Britain and consider options to address them. Issued Declaration of Resolves and agreed to meet again if nothing was solved.	King George was outraged and declared the New England colonies in rebellion. General Gage was ordered to put down the rebellion.
Paul Revere's Ride	1775	Fearing the British would seize colonial supplies and weapons and ammunition, Paul Revere was sent out on his famous ride through the Boston countryside to warn towns to turn on their militia and prevent this from happening.	Towns turned out their minutemen as militia prepared to confront the British.
Lexington and Concord	1775	General Gage dispatched British soldiers who marched toward Concord, Massachusetts where colonial munitions were stored. They were met on the village green in Lexington, Massachusetts by colonial minutemen.	The Redcoats ordered the militia to disperse, but they would not do so. Someone opened fire triggering the start of the Revolutionary War. It is not clear which side fired the shot later known as "the shot heard round the world."
Second Continental Congress	1775	All colonies sent delegates to Philadelphia in May 1775.	Congress authorized a Continental Army and put George Washington in command.
Olive Branch Petition	1775	After the Battle of Bunker Hill the Continental Congress issued the Olive Branch Petition to King George stating their loyalty and desire for peace and reconciliation with Britain.	King rejected this plea, sent the Royal Navy to blockade all shipping to the colonies and sent Hessian mercenaries to help the British defeat the colonists.

LESSON PLAN
AMERICAN REVOLUTION EXCEL PROJECT I

Teacher:	Date:
Subject:	Period(s):
Title of Lesson:	State Standards:
Common Core Standards and Indicators: **RH.9-10.7.** Integrate quantitative or technical analysis (e.g., charts, research data) with qualitative analysis in print or digital text **RH.11-12.7.** Integrate and evaluate multiple sources of information presented in diverse formats and media (e.g., visually, quantitatively, as well as in words) in order to address a question or solve a problem	College Readiness Standards: **ACT-CR: Reading, ACT-CR: Score Range 16–19** **Generalizations and Conclusions:** Draw simple generalizations and conclusions about people, ideas, and so on in uncomplicated passages

Purpose/ Objective	To enhance students' knowledge of the American Revolution while also teaching them how to use Microsoft Excel.
Materials	Project directions contained on the following page, textbook, Internet, other teacher-supplied resources, LCD projector, computer with Microsoft Excel
Procedures	Divide the students into cooperative groups and pass out copies of the directions for the project. Explain the directions. Display a sample Excel spreadsheet to the class using a computer and LCD projector. Explain how to set up the spreadsheet using the examples given on the second page of the directions. Explain the basic mathematical functions of Excel to students and show them some simple formulas. Students should take notes on how to set up their spreadsheet.
Assessment	Teacher will determine how many points this project is worth and can grade it using a rubric or a sliding scale.
Comments	Microsoft's Encarta encyclopedia used to have a great table with all of this information. Unfortunately, Encarta is now defunct, but an examination of the primary sources that contain this information could be a separate lesson unto itself. Otherwise, the teacher should analyze the sources cited for this activity and prepare a handout for the students that condenses the necessary information they will need to complete the project.

American Revolution Excel Project I

Microsoft Excel is an extremely powerful and versatile database program used by people all over the world. It has countless types of personal, business, and educational applications. Excel's pages, or spreadsheets, are used to collect, organize, manipulate, and display a variety of information. It is used to keep track of personal information such as names and addresses, which can be used to create letters and mailings. It is used to track business inventory, sort and calculate mathematical data, and keep lists of information that can be imported into other programs. Excel can also use the information in its database to create charts, graphs, and other graphic representations of information to facilitate the further analysis of the data.

"No taxation without representation" was the rallying call that went out as many colonists began to express their discontent with the new taxes imposed on them by England after the French and Indian War. In our class you are going to use Microsoft Excel to collect information on various taxes England levied on its American colonies then use the program to create charts or graphs to display how much revenue each tax generated.

Revenue-Raising Laws to Include: Sugar Act, Stamp Act, Townshend Acts

Resources/Websites: Historical Statistics of the U.S. Bureau of the Census; Encyclopedia of the North American Colonies; Blackwell Encyclopedia of the American Revolution

Steps:

1. Use the Internet to research the total amount of money collected from each tax. You will record this information on the Excel spreadsheet you will create.

2. Set up your Microsoft Excel spreadsheet categories (columns and rows) with the names of the taxes and the amount of money they generated (in British currency of the time). Include the date when the tax was created and when it was repealed.

3. Write a simple mathematical formula to make the program calculate the total amount of revenue generated by each tax.

4. Use the program to display the results on a chart or graph.

5. Use the charts and graphs to draw conclusions about the taxes and explain those conclusions to the class.

American Revolution Excel Project I

Sample Excel Spreadsheet

	A	B	C	D	F
1		Projected Revenue	Actual Revenue		
2	Sugar Act 1764				
3	Stamp Act 1765				
4	Townshend Acts 1767				
5	Total Revenue				

Analysis Questions

1. Did the actual revenue generated by each of the taxes match what Parliament expected to profit from the taxes?

2. Did the taxes generate more money for Parliament over time or less money, meaning were the taxes effective in raising a lot of money for England?

LESSON PLAN
FILM: "1776"

Teacher:	Date:
Subject:	Period(s):
Title of Lesson:	State Standards:
Common Core Standards and Indicators:	College Readiness Standards:

Purpose/ Objective	Students will gain a more in-depth knowledge of events surrounding the writing of the Declaration of Independence.
Materials	DVD of the movie *1776*, copies of film questions from the following page
Procedures	Before starting movie, asked students to recall for the class anything they know or remember about the Declaration of Independence. Give the students a brief overview of the movie and the central characters they will see in the film. Pass out copies of the questions and preview them with the students. Start the film but stop at key points to make comments, explain things, or check for student understanding by asking questions.
Assessment	Grade the film questions. Questions about the film or the Declaration of Independence can be included on a quiz or text. Students can be asked to write a summary of the movie.
Comments	As always, teacher should prepare for this activity by previewing the film before showing it to the class. This film does an excellent job at providing insights as to the various views surrounding the issue of independence, which should be emphasized and explained by teacher. Toward the end of the film the reasons slavery was not abolished right away are explained. Teacher should emphasize this as well as its relation to the song "Molasses to Rum." This film was originally written as a play. To save time, and student interest, some of the songs can be fast-forwarded through. It should take 3-4 days to show entire film depending how much of it the teacher skips.

Film Questions for "1776"

1. What colony does John Adams represent and what does he want the 2nd Continental Congress to vote on?
2. Who is the person having a portrait painted of himself?
3. Who came to see Adams and Franklin and what colony does he represent?
4. What does Ben Franklin want Richard Henry Lee to do in Congress?
5. What colony does Mr. Rutledge represent?
6. What colony does Mr. Dickinson represent?
7. Who is president of the 2nd Continental Congress?
8. What colony does Thomas Jefferson represent?
9. How does Mr. Dickinson feel about England? Would you consider him a patriot or loyalist?
10. How does John Adams feel about England? Would you consider him a patriot or loyalist?
11. What does Ben Franklin think about England and the American people?
12. Where does New Jersey stand on the question of independence?
13. What excuse does Adams give to postpone the vote on independence?
14. Who was picked to write the Declaration of Independence and why?
15. What colony does Ben Franklin represent?
16. How does George Washington describe the Continental Army?
17. Why did John Adams take Mr. Chase of Maryland to see the Continental Army?
18. What does the song "Cool, Cool, Considerate Men," led by Mr. Dickinson, tell you about many of these men and why they didn't want to support independence?
19. Why did Maryland finally decide to support independence?
20. Why did Jefferson consider King George a tyrant?
21. Why doesn't Mr. Rutledge of South Carolina like the Declaration? What did he want changed?
22. Is Jefferson in favor of slavery or against it? Why is this a hard issue for him?
23. What point was Rutledge making in the song "Molasses to Rum?" What was the song about?
24. What will it take to get South Carolina to agree to the Declaration of Independence?
25. Why did Adams and Jefferson finally agree to remove the slavery clause?
26. Who was the first person to sign the Declaration of Independence? Why did he write his name so large?

LESSON PLAN
GRAPHIC ORGANIZER
EVENTS OF THE AMERICAN REVOLUTION

Teacher:	Date:
Subject:	Period(s):
Title of Lesson:	State Standards:
Common Core Standards and Indicators: **RH.11-12.2.** Determine the central ideas or information of a primary or secondary source; provide an accurate summary that makes clear the relationships among the key details and ideas	College Readiness Standards: **ACT-CR: Reading, ACT-CR: Score Range 20–23** **Sequential, Comparative, and Cause-Effect Relationships**: Identify clear relationships between people, ideas, and so on in uncomplicated passages **ACT-CR: Reading, ACT-CR: Score Range 16–19** **Generalizations and Conclusions:** Draw simple generalizations and conclusions about people, ideas, and so on in uncomplicated passages

Purpose/ Objective	Students will gain a better understanding of the events of the American Revolution while enhancing their reading, writing, summarization, and critical thinking skills.
Materials	Copies of blank graphic organizer contained on following pages, transparency of graphic organizer completed with possible answers contained on following pages, textbook or other sources such as the Internet
Procedures	Teacher will distribute blank copies of graphic organizer to students and explain the assignment. Students are to use their textbook or other sources to complete the graphic organizer. When the assignment is completed teacher should display the transparency of the completed graphic organizer on the overhead projector and go over possible answers with the students so they can check their work.
Assessment	Assignment can be graded on a standard scale with points taken off for each item missed or a rubric can be designed. Students will be quizzed and tested on this information. The information from this activity can be used for other activities, such as the American Revolution PowerPoint project.
Comments	Teacher can collect and grade the assignment before going over the answers or give the students a chance to correct their work by going over the answers with the students before the assignment is collected. This is always at the teacher's discretion and depends on the level of the students and difficulty of assignment. The completed graphic organizer can also be used simply as handout notes or as lecture notes.

Events of the American Revolution

Name____________________________

Event	Date	Location	Importance
Capture of Fort Ticonderoga			
The Battle of Bunker Hill			
Battle of Quebec			
The British leave Boston			
The Fight over the Carolinas			
"Common Sense" is published			

Event	Date	Location	Importance
The Declaration of Independence			
Battle of Brooklyn Heights			
Battle of White Plains			
Battle of Trenton			
Battle of Saratoga			
Winter at Valley Forge			

Event	Date	Location	Importance
Bonhomme Richard v. the *Serapis*			
Battle of Vincennes			
Battle of Monmouth			
Battle of Charleston			
Battle of Camden			
Battle of King's Mountain			

Event	Date	Location	Importance
Treason of Benedict Arnold			
The Morris Town Mutiny			
Battle of Yorktown			
Treaty of Paris			

Events of the American Revolution

Name______________________________

Event	Date	Location	Importance
Capture of Fort Ticonderoga	May 10, 1775	150 miles outside Boston	Led by Ethan Allen and Benedict Arnold. Victory gave colonists confidence while also capturing weapons and canons.
The Battle of Bunker Hill	June 17, 1775	Breeds Hill/Bunker Hill outside of Boston	Colonists lost but gained confidence by holding off British advances. British suffered more casualties but showed their resolve. "Don't one of you fire until you see the whites of their eyes" was an order given by an American commander to save ammunition.
Battle of Quebec	December 31,1775	Quebec, Canada	Colonists lost and did not get any support from the Canadians like they thought they would.
The British leave Boston	March 1776	Boston, Massachusetts	Colonists took Boston without a fight. British retreated because of the canons on Dorchester Heights.
The Fight over the Carolinas	February 1776	North and South Carolina	British thought it would be an easy victory. British retreated to North Carolina.
"Common Sense" is published	January 1776	Philadelphia, Pennsylvania	Thomas Paine wrote this pamphlet convincing people independence made sense and was the right thing for the colonies to do. Over 120,000 copies were printed.

Event	Date	Location	Importance
The Declaration of Independence	July 4, 1776	Philadelphia, Pennsylvania	Document that declared American independence and convinced more people to join the cause for independence. Outlined principles of independence and relationship of government to its people.
Battle of Brooklyn Heights	August 27, 1776	New York	First major battle after United States declared itself its own nation. Major defeat in which the Continental Army was eventually forced to retreat into New Jersey and Pennsylvania.
Battle of White Plains	September 1776	New York	Indecisive battle but caused Americans to retreat across New Jersey into Pennsylvania. Separated British Army from Continental Army by Delaware River.
Battle of Trenton	December 25, 1776	Trenton, New Jersey	George Washington led Continental Army across Delaware River to take Trenton. Captured 900 Hessian mercenaries.
Battle of Saratoga	September 1777	Saratoga, New York	American victory and turning point of war. Militia turned back General Burgoyne's army, which led to his surrender. Victory convinced France and Spain to help the Americans.
Winter at Valley Forge	Winter 1777-1778	20 miles outside Philadelphia, Pennsylvania	Period of suffering for Continental Army. George Washington credited with keeping his troops together during period of cold, sickness, lack of food, low morale. Continental Army retrained by Baron Von Steuben in spring of 1778.

Event	Date	Location	Importance
Bonhomme Richard v. the *Serapis*	1779	Off the English coast	Sea battle in which American commander John Paul Jones and his ship, the *Bonhomme Richard*, forced the British ship, the *Serapis* to surrender. Earned Jones the reputation of America's first well-known naval fighter.
Battle of Vincennes	July 4, 1778 and February 1779	Illinois	French settlers helped Colonel George Rogers Clark capture Cahokia and Vincennes. Recaptured by British then took again in 1779 by Colonel Clark. Left Americans in control of Northwest Territory.
Battle of Monmouth	Summer 1779	New Jersey	Not a decisive victory but kept British in area until the end of war. British went to New York and George Washington and his men to New Jersey.
Battle of Charleston	May 1780	Charleston, South Carolina	British General Clinton and British fleet forced the surrender of Charleston. About 5,000 American soldiers captured, the biggest troop loss of the war.
Battle of Camden	August 1780	Camden, South Carolina	Major British victory by Lord Cornwallis over the American General Horatio Gates in which he strengthened the British hold on the Carolinas.
Battle of King's Mountain	October 1780	Western border of North and South Carolina	Western Patriot guerilla fighters forced loyalist surrender.

Event	Date	Location	Importance
Treason of Benedict Arnold	Fall of 1780	New York	General Arnold agreed to turn over fort to British in return for money and commission as Brigadier General. Plot discovered but Arnold escaped.
The Morris Town Mutiny	1781	New Jersey	Pennsylvania soldiers mutinied over lack of pay and length of service. Men were promised their back pay and were released.
Battle of Yorktown	October 19, 1781	Yorktown, Virginia	Final major battle of the war. General Washington pinned General Cornwallis and his men in against the sea where they were also boxed in by the French fleet. Cornwallis surrendered as a band reportedly played an old English folk tune, the "World Turned Upside Down."
Treaty of Paris	September 3, 1783	Paris, France	Peace treaty that ended the war and officially recognized American independence. Also outlined the boundaries of the United States from Canada south to Florida and west to the Mississippi River.

LESSON PLAN
AMERICAN REVOLUTION EXCEL PROJECT II

Teacher:	Date:
Subject:	Period(s):
Title of Lesson:	State Standards:
Common Core Standards and Indicators: **RH.9-10.7.** Integrate quantitative or technical analysis (e.g., charts, research data) with qualitative analysis in print or digital text **RH.11-12.7.** Integrate and evaluate multiple sources of information presented in diverse formats and media (e.g., visually, quantitatively, as well as in words) in order to address a question or solve a problem	College Readiness Standards: **ACT-CR: Reading, ACT-CR: Score Range 16–19 Generalizations and Conclusions:** Draw simple generalizations and conclusions about people, ideas, and so on in uncomplicated passages

Purpose/ Objective	To enhance students' knowledge of the American Revolution while also teaching them how to use Microsoft Excel.
Materials	Project directions contained on the following pages, textbook, Internet, other teacher-supplied resources, LCD projector, computer with Microsoft Excel
Procedures	Divide the students into cooperative groups. Pass out copies of directions for the project. Explain the directions. Display a sample Excel spreadsheet to the class using a computer and LCD projector. Explain how to set up the spreadsheet using the examples given on the second page of the directions. Explain the basic mathematical functions of Excel to students and show them some simple formulas. Students should take notes on how to set up their spreadsheet.
Assessment	Teacher will determine how many points this project is worth and can grade it using a rubric or a sliding scale.
Comments	A working knowledge of Excel is required by the teacher. Examples of how to set up the spreadsheet are included with the directions, but the mathematical formulas are not. Figuring out how to write the formulas in the proper cells will be part of the students' learning curve though the teacher should help them with this by giving them some examples.

American Revolution Excel Project II

Microsoft Excel is an extremely powerful and versatile database program used by people all over the world. It has countless types of personal, business, and educational applications. Excel's pages, or spreadsheets, are used to collect, organize, manipulate, and display a variety of information. It is used to keep track of personal information such as names and addresses, which can be used to create letters and mailings. It is used to track business inventory, sort and calculate mathematical data, and keep lists of information that can be imported into other programs. Excel can also use the information in its database to create charts, graphs, and other graphic representations of information to facilitate the further analysis of the data.

In our class you are going to use Microsoft Excel to collect information on various battles of the American Revolution then use the program to create charts or graphs that display battlefield information, such as the number of casualties each side suffered. Once your teacher shows you how to set up the Excel spreadsheet you are to enter the required battlefield information you will research on a spreadsheet then graph the results.

Websites: theamericanrevolution.org/battles, wikipedia.com (search for the individual battles)

Battles to Include: Lexington and Concord, Bunker Hill, Trenton, Saratoga, Camden, Yorktown

Steps:

1. Research the total number of soldiers engaged and the total casualties for each battle for the Colonials and the British. Record the information on the spreadsheet.
2. Set up your Microsoft Excel categories (columns and rows) with the total number engaged and the total casualties for the each side using the information you have already collected. Include the location and the date for each battle.
3. Write a simple mathematical formula to make the program calculate the total loses in each category for each side and for each battle.
4. Use the program to display the results on a chart or graph.
5. Use the graphs and analysis questions to draw conclusions about the battles and explain those conclusions to the class.

American Revolution Excel Project II

Sample Excel Spreadsheet

	A	B	C	D	F
1		Total Colonials Engaged	Total Colonial Casualties	Total British Engaged	Total British Casualties
2	Lexington (April 1775)				
3	Bunker Hill (June 1775)				
4	Trenton (December 1776)				
5	Saratoga (September-October 1777)				
6	Camden (August 1780)				
7	Yorktown (October 1781)				

Analysis Questions

1. Which side had more troops engaged in battles earlier in the war?

2. Was this advantage maintained throughout the war?

3. Which side suffered more losses in all of these battles combined?

American Revolution Timeline Activity

Directions: Place each of the following items in correct chronological order on a timeline. Write the date of the event above the timeline and the name of the event below the timeline along with a short description of the event and/or short explanation of why it was important.

French and Indian War
Albany Plan of Union
Treaty of Paris of 1763
Intolerable Acts
Sugar Act
Proclamation of 1763
Stamp Act
Boston Massacre
Boston Tea Party
Formation of the Sons of Liberty
Townshend Acts
Quartering Act
Stamp Act Congress
Quebec Act
"Shot heard around the world"
First Continental Congress
Declaration of Resolves
Second Continental Congress
Establishment of the Continental Army
Olive Branch Petition
King George III sent Hessian troops to fight the Americans
Declaration of Independence
Declaratory Act
Battle of Bunker Hill/Breeds Hill
Speech by Patrick Henry
Thomas Paine published "Common Sense"
Washington crossed the Delaware River and the Battle of Trenton
Battle of Saratoga
Valley Forge
Battle of Yorktown
Treat of Paris of 1783

LESSON PLAN
AMERICAN REVOLUTION POWERPOINT PROJECT

Teacher:	Date:
Subject:	Period(s):
Title of Lesson:	State Standards:
Common Core Standards and Indicators: **RH.11-12.2.** Determine the central ideas or information of a primary or secondary source; provide an accurate summary that makes clear the relationships among the key details and ideas	College Readiness Standards: **ACT-CR: Reading, ACT-CR: Score Range 16–19 Generalizations and Conclusions:** Draw simple generalizations and conclusions about people, ideas, and so on in uncomplicated passages

Purpose/ Objective	To enhance students' knowledge of the American Revolution through the use of Microsoft PowerPoint while also enhancing their presentation skills.
Materials	Project directions contained on following page; textbook; Internet; notes, graphic organizers, and any other materials used in the students' study of the American Revolution; computer and LCD projector
Procedures	Divide class into cooperative groups. Pass out and explain project directions and grading scale. Show students the basics of using PowerPoint such as how to choose slide layouts and backgrounds, slide transitions, special effects, etc. Using computer and LCD projector show students examples of good PowerPoint slides for this project.
Assessment	Project can be graded using the sample rubric provided or teacher can create a more detailed rubric.
Comments	A basic working knowledge of PowerPoint is required by teacher. Do not assume all students know how to use PowerPoint. Give students a couple weeks to work on this project then have them present their projects to the class. Projects can be emailed to the teacher by assigned due date for grading. Consider an optional presentation grade.

American Independence PowerPoint Project

You are a famous Hollywood producer, and you have just been hired to make a movie about the United States and its road to independence. Work in groups of four to five to display all of your knowledge about the events that led the English colonies to break away from England and ultimately obtain their independence. Movies are first made by creating a storyboard of events that explain what is going to happen in the movie. Your storyboard should be a slideshow of the information and images you are going to include in the movie.

Each slide should focus on one event or item and have a date and title at the top. Each slide should also have some type of photo or image that represents the event and a brief summary explaining the event. As a good producer you will want to cover all the main characters (Franklin, Washington, Jefferson, Adams, King of England, etc.) and important events from start to finish. Start with one slide about life in the English colonies (include a map of the colonies) before 1754 then move on to explain the changes that took place after the French and Indian War that led to increased British control over the colonies and greater taxation. Groups will present their slideshows to the class.

Events to Include

Colonial life/indentured servitude
Theory of mercantilism
Navigation Acts
French and Indian War
Albany Plan of Union
Proclamation of 1763
Sugar Act
Stamp Act
Quartering Act
Sam Adams & Sons of Liberty
"Taxation without representation"
Non-importation Agreements
Stamp Act Congress
Declaratory Act
Townshend Acts
Boston Massacre
Tea Act/Boston Tea Party
Intolerable Acts (4parts
Quebec Act
First Continental Congress
Militias & Minutemen
Paul Revere's Midnight Ride
"Shot heard around the world"
Second Continental Congress
Patriots & Loyalists
Patrick Henry
Thomas Paine /"Common Sense"
Thomas Jefferson
Declaration of Independence
Important Battles/Treaty of Paris

Group Members____

Grading Scale

Categories	**Points Possible**	**Points Earned**
Completion of all slides	**25**	
Accuracy of information	**25**	
Creativity	**25**	
Overall presentation	**25**	
Total	**100**	

Name______________________

American Independence Test

Multiple Choice

1. As a result of the French and Indian War
   a) France lost Canada
   b) England lost Canada
   c) France taxed the colonies more
   d) none of the above

2. French and Indian War was important because
   a) it led to more control and taxation of the colonies by England
   b) it led to more control and taxation of the colonies by France
   c) caused the colonies to lose a lot of land
   d) got the colonies to cooperate with each other

3. A term for a harsh and unfair ruler is
   a) tyrant b) benefactor c) monarch d) minuteman

4. The Albany Plan of Union called for the
   a) overthrow of the king
   b) destruction of the French Empire
   c) establishing colonial cooperation
   d) establishing an official religion

5. Who won in the French and Indian War?
   a) France b) Indians c) England d) France and the Indians

6. Colonists thought the Stamp Act was
   a) not that bad
   b) taxation without representation
   c) a small price to pay for postal service
   d) a good way to raise money

7. What resulted in the Boston Tea Party?
   a) Intolerable Acts b) Tea Act c) Sugar Act d) Townshend Act

8. As a result of the Boston Tea Party England passed the
   a) Declaratory Act b) Boston Massacre c) Currency Act d) Intolerable Acts

9. What was the Quartering Act?
   a) said colonists must serve in the British army
   b) said colonists must serve in their local militia
   c) said colonies had to house and feed British soldiers
   d) created a new 25-cent coin

10. The Intolerable Acts
    a) forced colonists to pay for their own defense
    b) increased colonial trade
    c) resulted in the Boston Massacre
    d) punished Boston for the "Tea Party"

11. Who said "Give me liberty or give me death?"
    a) Paul Revere   b) Patrick Henry   c) Sam Adams   d) Ben Franklin

12. The first battles for independence were fought in which colony?
    a) Virginia   b) Maryland   c) South Carolina   d) Massachusetts

13. Who organized the Sons of Liberty in Boston?
    a) Paul Revere   b) Patrick Henry   c) Sam Adams   d) Ben Franklin

14. The Proclamation of 1763 prohibited
    a) settlement west of the Appalachian Mountains
    b) taxes on sugar
    c) taxes on all imports
    d) none of the above

15. Who wrote the pamphlet "Common Sense?"
    a) Ben Franklin   b) Patrick Henry   c) John Adams   d) Thomas Paine

16. When the Declaration of Independence was signed on July 4, 1776, the Revolutionary War was over
    a) True   b) False

17. The image represents which event or item?
    a) Albany Plan of Union   b) Boston Massacre   c) Boston Tea Party   d) Shot heard around the world

18. This image represents which event or item?
    a) Albany Plan of Union   b) Sons of Liberty   c) Paul Revere's ride   d) Shot heard around the world

19. What group issued the Declaration of Independence?
    a) Sons of Liberty b) Stamp Act Congress c) 1st Continental Congress d) 2nd Continental Congress

20. The Declaration of Independence is broken down into how many parts?
    a) four b) three c) five d) six

Matching

21. General of the Continental Army	A) Patriots
22. Mercenaries hired by the British	B) John Hancock
23. People who supported independence	C) Loyalists
24. People who were against independence	D) George Washington
25. President of the 2nd Continental Congress	E) Hessians

Matching

26. King of England	A) Redcoat
27. Warrants to search for smuggled goods	B) Prudence
28. British soldier	C) Endowed
29. Common sense or wisdom	D) George III
30. To be given something	E) Writs of Assistance

Matching

31. Location of shot heard round the world	A) Yorktown
32. Turning point of war	B) Olive Branch Petition
33. Period of suffering for Continental Army	C) Saratoga
34. Last major battle of the war	D) Lexington
35. Last attempt to make peace with England	E) Valley Forge

Matching

36. Ended war and recognized American independence
37. "Don't shoot 'til you see the whites of their eyes"
38. American traitor
39. Member of the colonial militia
40. Responsible for the Boston Tea Party

A) Minutemen
B) Benedict Arnold
C) Treaty of Paris
D) Bunker's Hill/Breeds Hill
E) Sons of Liberty

Matching

41. Polish military officer who trained Americans
42. Secret society who opposed British policies
43. Tax on printed materials
44. Said "We must all hang together or hang separately"
45. British General who surrendered at Yorktown

A) Ben Franklin
B) Sons of Liberty
C) Casimir Pulaski
D) Stamp Act
E) Charles Cornwallis

Short Answer (answer on separate sheet of paper)

46. What unalienable rights did Jefferson mention in the Declaration of Independence?

47. Explain what the colonists meant by "taxation without representation."

48. Explain the arguments in favor and against independence.

49. Explain how the Enlightenment influenced the American Revolution.

50. Explain how the colonists responded to the Stamp Act.

Articles of Confederation

- 1st form of government in the U.S. was the Articles of Confederation
- Designed to be a weak government to avoid abuse of power
- Favored states' rights over federal (national) power
- Articles were proposed July 12, 1776 and adopted on November 15, 1777
- Created a loose confederation of states that guaranteed the *sovereignty* of each state
- Officially ratified in 1781 and used until the Constitution was adopted

Provisions of the Articles of Confederation

- Borrow and coin money
- Conduct foreign affairs
- Set Indian policy
- Settle disputes between states
- Each state had one vote in Congress
- To regulate distribution of land Congress passed the **Land Ordinance of 1785**, which divided land into townships of 640-acre tracks with one section set aside for the establishment of a school
- Also passed the **Northwest Ordinance** (1787) to establish system for governing the Northwest Territory (WI,MI,IL,IN,OH) and outlined the steps necessary to achieve statehood while prohibiting slavery in the area

Weakness of the Articles of Confederation

- Changes required the consent of all 13 states
- Major laws required consent of 9 states
- No power to tax or regulate commerce (trade)
- No national court system
- No central leader (president)
- Only a legislative body

Shay's Rebellion in Massachusetts in 1786, highlighted the problems with the Articles of Confederation and prompted a call to address the issues, which led to the Constitutional Convention in 1787.

Constitutional Convention

- Constitutional Convention began in May 1787 in Philadelphia to "fix" Articles of Confederation
- George Washington was selected to be the presiding officer. Thomas Jefferson and John Adams were in Europe, and Patrick Henry "smelled a rat"
- James Madison (known as the Father of the Constitution) proposed a radically new idea
- Madison proposed the **Virginia Plan**
- Since the Virginia Plan shifted power toward a central government, the plan reflected Madison's belief in ***federalism*****, where powers of government are divided between states and the federal government**
- The Virginia Plan also called for the creation of three branches of government, a ***bicameral*** legislature, and would give Congress the right to overturn state laws
- The Virginia Plan called for representation in Congress based on population
- Smaller states did not like this so W. Patterson proposed the **New Jersey** Plan, which called for representation based on an equal vote for each state

The Great Compromise

- To end the debate over representation in Congress, Roger Sherman of Connecticut proposed a bicameral legislature with one legislative house based on population (House of Representatives) and one legislative house based on equal representation for each state (Senate)
- This proposal is known as the **Great Compromise**

Constitutional Convention

Three-Fifths Compromise

- **The 3/5 Compromise** was reached to settle the dispute between northern and southern states as to how to count slaves as part of the population
- Compromise stated that 3 out of every 5 slaves would be included in a state's population for purposes of representation in Congress

Commerce Compromise

- Southern states feared the federal government would impose *tariffs* (taxes on imports and exports) that would hurt the sale of their goods overseas
- Southerners also feared the federal government would impose high tariffs on slaves to restrict the slave trade
- The Compromise only allowed the government to tax imports and would end the importation of slaves in 1807 but give slave holders the right to pursue runaway slaves across state lines
- Many northerners agreed to the Compromise to preserve the Union; they also thought slavery was a dying institution

Constitutional Convention

Ratification of the Constitution

- The new Constitution was signed by the delegates of the 13 states on September 17, 1787, but it still had to be *ratified* by all the states
- Ratification required approval of 9/13 states
- Those who favored the Constitution and a strong central government were called **Federalists**, such as James Madison, Alexander Hamilton, and John Jay
- Those who favored a weaker government and did not support the Constitution were called **Anti-Federalists**, such as Patrick Henry
- Jay, Madison, and Hamilton won support for the Constitution by publishing a series of 85 essays called the **Federalist Papers**
- The Anti-Federalists would not support the Constitution until it was agreed a **Bill of Rights** would be added as the first act of Congress
    - The Bill of Rights are the first ten amendments to the Constitution and protect our most cherished freedoms as Americans
- The Constitution was finally ratified in 1788 and the Bill of Rights in 1791
- The differences between the Federalists and Anti-Federalists later laid the foundations for the creation of the first political parties
- Most of the delegates were wealthy men actually able to loan the government money themselves
- There was a general mistrust of the common man, who were supported by people like Jefferson and Henry, but they were not at the Convention
- Many of the most democratic features of the Constitution were added over the years
- Originally, only white, male landowners could vote

Framework of the Constitution

Separation of Powers

- To keep the government from becoming too powerful the powers of the government were divided among three different branches
  - Legislative Branch-makes the laws
  - Executive Branch-enforces or carries out the laws
  - Judicial Branch-administers justice through a court system and interprets laws

Checks and Balances

- To keep any one branch from becoming more powerful than the others a system of checks and balances was created that gives each branch the means to restrain the other two
- Checks and balances upholds the concept of separation of powers

Organization of the Constitution

- The Three Parts of the Constitution
  - Preamble-lists the six goals of the Constitution

  - Seven Articles-provides the framework of the Constitution
    - Article I-The Legislative Branch
    - Article II-The Executive Branch
    - Article III-The Judicial Branch
    - Article IV-Relations and Equality Among the States
    - Article V-Procedures for amending the Constitution
    - Article VI-The Role of the National Government
    - Article VII-Ratification of the Constitution

  - Amendments-27 changes or additions to the original Constitution

The Legislative Branch

The Legislative Branch

- Purpose is to make laws
- Also known as Congress
- Meets in the Capitol Building
- Bicameral (two houses)-Senate and House of Representatives

The Senate

- Two senators from each state (100 total)
- Pass bills
- Approve treaties
- Approve Presidential appointments
- Acts as jury in impeachment trials
- Vice-President of U.S. acts as president (presiding officer) of Senate
- Elect President Pro Tempore
- Elected for 6-year terms, with no term limits
- 1/3 of Senators are up for election each time to stagger experience in Congress

Qualifications to Become a Senator

- 30 years old
- Live in state represented
- Citizen of U.S. for 9 years
- Vacancies filled by state's governor appointing a temporary senator
- $168,500 annual salary

The House of Representatives

- Number of representatives from each state determined by state's population
- 435 total members in House (set by law)
- Speaker of the House is the presiding officer
- Pass bills
- Must start all revenue laws (money/tax laws)
- Bring charges of impeachment
- Selects president if no candidate receives a majority of electoral votes in an election
- Elected for 2-year terms, with no term limits

- Elected every two years and take office January 3rd after the November election

Qualifications to Become of a Member of the House of Representatives

- 25 years old
- Live in state represented
- Citizen of U.S. for 7 years
- Vacancies filled by a special election called by state's governor
- $168,500 annual salary

Powers of Congress

<u>Expressed, Delegated, Enumerated Powers (powers of federal government)</u>

- Coin money
- Establish postal service
- Regulate interstate and foreign trade
- Register copyrights and patents
- Set standard weights and measures
- Establish foreign policy
- Raise and support armed forces
- Make war and peace
- Regulate immigration and naturalization
- Create all necessary laws for carrying out delegated powers

<u>Reserved Powers (state powers)</u>

- Establish local governments
- Establish schools
- Regulate business within state
- Charter corporations
- Regulate labor, business, marriage/divorce laws
- Conduct elections
- Provide for public safety
- Assume other powers not delegated to the national government or not prohibited to the states

<u>Concurrent Powers (shared powers)</u>

- Maintain law and order
- Levy taxes
- Borrow money
- Charter banks
- Establish courts
- Provide for the public welfare

<u>Implied Powers</u>-powers not written in the Constitution but believed the government has

Certain Powers Granted or Denied Congress

- Congress governs Washington D.C. (District of Columbia) for all of America
- Elastic Clause (Necessary and Proper Clause)-stretch powers to create new laws when necessary to carry out functions of government
- No ex post facto laws-laws made after the fact
- Cannot suspend right of Habeas Corpus except under special circumstances- must bring prisoner before judge to be accused of a crime

The Executive Branch

The Executive Branch

- Job is to enforce or carry out the country's laws
- President, Vice-president, Cabinet (15 advisors)

President

- Considered the commander-in-chief of the armed forces
- Limit of **two terms** of 4 years each or maximum of 10 years total
- Must be 35 years old
- Natural born citizen
- Lived in country for 14 years
- Takes oath of office January 20th
- Appoints officials in the Executive and Judicial Branches
- Appoints federal and Supreme Court judges (with Senate approval)
- Prepares the federal budget every year
- Salary is $400,000
- President > Vice-President> Speaker of the House> President Pro Tempore> Secretary of State, etc.

Vice-President

- Same requirements to hold office
- Acts as president of Senate; only votes to break a tie
- Salary is $212,000
- In case of vacancy, President appoints a new Vice-President (approved by Congress)

Electoral College

- Originally created due to the Framers distrust of the average person but also a way to boost the voting power of the smaller, less populated states
- Group of people appointed by state legislatures who actually vote for president
- Generally, the candidate who receives the most popular votes in a state gets that state's electoral votes
- Each state's electoral votes is equal to the total number of people each state has in Congress (senators + house members)
- 538 electoral votes possible (435+100+ 3 for Washington D.C.)
- Candidate needs 270 electoral votes to win, otherwise the House of Representatives chooses the president

The Judicial Branch

Judicial Branch

- Primary purpose is to administer justice through a federal court system
- Also interprets laws through a process called **judicial review** (decides if laws are constitutional or not)
- Process of judicial review first established in 1803 in case of *Marbury v. Madison*
- Comprised of three levels of federal courts

Supreme Court

- Highest court in the land
- Meets in Supreme Court building in Washington D.C.
- Currently 9 justices (judges)
- Appointed for life by the president (need Senate approval)
- Chief Justice is head of Supreme Court
- Hears federal and constitutional cases and those appealed from lower courts
- Salary is $203,000 ($212,100 for Chief Justice)

Court of Appeals

- 13 appellate courts with 3 to 9 judges
- Hears cases from lower courts that can be appealed for review
- Meet in the various circuits
- Created in 1891 to relieve the Supreme Court

District Courts

- Ordinary trial courts for federal laws/issues
- 94 district courts across the country with 1 to 24 judges
- Meet in the various districts

Constitution Review Sheet

1. Our government is based on the idea of democracy. What is a true democracy and how is it different from a republic? Which one is our Constitution modeled after?
___
___
___

2. The Articles of Confederation was the country's first form of government. What was the problem(s) with the Articles that led to the creation of the Constitution?
___

3. During the Constitutional Convention of 1787, the Great Compromise solved one of the biggest disagreements among the framers of the Constitution. What problem or issue did the Great Compromise solve? ___

4. The issue of whether or not slaves should be included in a state's population for purposes of representation in Congress was resolved with what other famous compromise?
___

5. What was the major disagreement between Federalists and Anti-Federalists?
___

6. What is the Bill of Rights and why was in put into the Constitution?
___

7. The Constitution is divided into three parts (not the branches). What are they?
___

8. What information is contained in the Preamble? ___

9. Explain the concepts of separation of powers and checks and balances.
___
___

10. The powers of the federal government are divided into three branches. What are they?
___

11. Who makes up the Legislative branch and what is its purpose?

____

12. Who makes up the Executive branch and what is its purpose?

____

13. Who makes up the Judicial branch and what is its purpose(s)?

____

14. Explain the concept of Federalism.

____

15. What are delegated, reserved, and concurrent powers? List three of each.

____

____

16. What is the difference between enumerated and implied powers?

____

17. What is the elastic clause? ______________________________

18. What is the Supremacy clause? ____________________________

19. List the requirements to hold office for a Senator, House of Representative member, and president.

____

____

20. List three powers and three duties of the Senate and the House.

____

____

Amendments

Focus on the following amendments:

1-10; 13-15; 16; 17; 18; 19; 20; 21; 22; 25; 26

LESSON PLAN
CONSTITUTION JEOPARDY PROJECT

Teacher:		Date:
Subject:		Period(s):
Title of Lesson:		State Standards:
Common Core Standards and Indicators: **RH.11-12.2.** Determine the central ideas or information of a primary or secondary source; provide an accurate summary that makes clear the relationships among the key details and ideas		College Readiness Standards: **ACT-CR: Reading, ACT-CR: Score Range 16–19** **Generalizations and Conclusions:** Draw simple generalizations and conclusions about people, ideas, and so on in uncomplicated passages
Purpose/ Objective	To help students prepare for the Constitution test while engaging them in a creative cooperative learning project. To use technology to enhance students' presentation abilities.	
Materials	Project directions and grading scale, Microsoft PowerPoint, textbook, Constitution materials, Internet, computer, LCD projector	
Procedures	Divide the class into cooperative learning groups. Pass out project directions and project grading scale (two project rubrics are contained on one page to save paper). Show students examples of how to use the jeopardy template using the computer and LCD projector. Make sure all students have teacher's email. Ask each group leader to email the teacher who will reply with a jeopardy template. Have students write their names on project grading scale (one per group) and return to teacher. Have students email projects to teacher according to due date. View projects on the computer and record grade on each group's grading slip.	
Assessment	A simple project rubric follows the project directions on the following page.	
Comments	There are several jeopardy templates available online that can be used or one can be made from scratch from within PowerPoint. Allow students to present their projects to the class. This will also serve as a review for the Constitution test. Teacher can also grade projects as they are presented to class.	

Jeopardy Constitution Project

You are to create a Jeopardy game with categories (and their questions and answers) related to the United States Constitution. You must have five categories such as, the Executive Branch, Legislative Branch, Judicial Branch, Requirements to Hold Office, Vacancies, etc., and a fun category such as Sports, Music or Movies.

Each category must have five questions with corresponding number values (100-500). Other possible categories include: Amendments, Powers of Congress, or Checks and Balances.

This is a group project. Projects must be done using Microsoft PowerPoint. I will email each group leader the blank template for PowerPoint Jeopardy that will be used to complete the project. The purpose of this project is to help you study for the Constitution test. Groups will be required to present their project to the class. This will also serve as a review for everyone. All finished projects must be emailed to ____________________ at ________________________. This assignment is due ______________.

Jeopardy Constitution Project

You are to create a Jeopardy game with categories (and their questions and answers) related to the United States Constitution. You must have five categories such as, the Executive Branch, Legislative Branch, Judicial Branch, Requirements to Hold Office, Vacancies, etc., and a fun category such as Sports, Music or Movies.

Each category must have five questions with corresponding number values (100-500). Other possible categories include: Amendments, Powers of Congress, or Checks and Balances.

This is a group project. Projects must be done using Microsoft PowerPoint. I will email each group leader the blank template for PowerPoint Jeopardy that will be used to complete the project. The purpose of this project is to help you study for the Constitution test. Groups will be required to present their project to the class. This will also serve as a review for everyone. All finished projects must be emailed to _________________ at ___________________________.This assignment is due ______________.

Constitution Jeopardy Project Rubric

Name______________________________ Period__________ Date_________________

Grading Rubric

Accuracy of information (20pts.) __________

Creativity (20pts.) __________

Included all required information (20pts.) __________

Effort and followed all directions (20pts.) __________

Overall effectiveness of presentation (20pts.) __________

Total points =100

Your score __________

Comments:

____

____

____

____

Constitution Jeopardy Project Rubric

Name______________________________ Period__________ Date_________________

Grading Rubric

Accuracy of information (20pts.) __________

Creativity (20pts.) __________

Included all required information (20pts.) __________

Effort and followed all directions (20pts.) __________

Overall effectiveness of presentation (20pts.) __________

Total points =100

Your score __________

Comments:

____

____

____

____

LESSON PLAN
OPPOSING VIEWS
WRITING ASSIGNMENT ON VOTING RIGHTS

Teacher:	Date:
Subject:	Period(s):
Title of Lesson:	State Standards:
Common Core Standards and Indicators: **RH.11-12.6.** Evaluate authors' differing points of view on the same historical event or issue by assessing the authors' claims, reasoning, and evidence. **WHST.11-12.1b.** Develop claim(s) and counterclaims fairly and thoroughly, supplying the most relevant data and evidence for each while pointing out the strengths and limitations of both claim(s) and counterclaims in a discipline-appropriate form that anticipates the audience's knowledge level, concerns, values, and possible biases	College Readiness Standards: **ACT-CR: Reading, ACT-CR: Score Range 20–23** **Generalizations and Conclusions:** Draw simple generalizations and conclusions using details that support the main points of more challenging passages

Purpose/ Objective	Students will learn more about the decision to limit voting rights to white, male landowners early in country's history and be given an opportunity to express their opinions on this issue, both pro and con, while enhancing their reading and writing skills through the evaluation of information.
Materials	Assignment directions and grading scale, pro and con articles on suffrage rights from *Opposing Views in American History, Volume I* or other sources
Procedures	Copy and pass out assignment directions and assignment grading scale. Explain directions to students. Start off with an overview of suffrage rights and how they were once restricted to white, male landowners. Explain why this happened and include the differing opinions of Jefferson and Hamilton as to whom should hold political power. Allow students ample class time to work on this so teacher can help them both with the writing and the reading of materials.
Assessment	Use the grading rubric included with this activity or teacher can design a new one.
Comments	The articles in *Opposing Views in American History, Volume I*, by William Dudley and published by Greenhaven Press were used for this assignment. They provide excellent and thought-provoking articles on controversial issues in American history. Since the democratic process, including voting rights, was extended to more people in the future, particularly during Andrew Jackson's presidency, this assignment is also relevant to the study of the Jacksonian era.

Writing Assignment: Opposing Views in American History

You are to read the handout that explains the different viewpoints on suffrage rights (voting rights) that existed when the United States was still a very young country. The fight over suffrage for different groups of people, particularly African Americans and women, continued for many years into our country's future, but initially, the right to vote was only given to white, male landowners. Some people were in favor of this; others thought the property ownership restriction should be removed. You are to write an essay in which you summarize the different points of view regarding early suffrage rights. **First,** start your essay off with an introduction that briefly explains the restrictions put on voting for different groups of people. **Second,** in the body of the essay, summarize the different viewpoints on suffrage rights as explained in the handouts. **Be sure to include the major reasons given to support each side. In your conclusion,** restate the two opposing viewpoints and explain which view had the best argument. Explain which view you agree with and why, as well as how voting restrictions placed on various people were in opposition to our country's founding ideas of democracy and equality. Before writing it is a good idea to start off with an outline that includes the information you will put in your essay and the order in which it will be written. All rules of standard written English apply. Your paper should be typed using 10-12 size font. Your grading scale is on the back.

Writing Assignment: Opposing Views in American History

You are to read the handout that explains the different viewpoints on suffrage rights (voting rights) that existed when the United States was still a very young country. The fight over suffrage for different groups of people, particularly African Americans and women, continued for many years into our country's future, but initially, the right to vote was only given to white, male landowners. Some people were in favor of this; others thought the property ownership restriction should be removed. You are to write an essay in which you summarize the different points of view regarding early suffrage rights. **First,** start your essay off with an introduction that briefly explains the restrictions put on voting for different groups of people. **Second,** in the body of the essay, summarize the different viewpoints on suffrage rights as explained in the handouts. **Be sure to include the major reasons given to support each side. In your conclusion,** restate the two opposing viewpoints and explain which view had the best argument. Explain which view you agree with and why, as well as how voting restrictions placed on various people were in opposition to our country's founding ideas of democracy and equality. Before writing it is a good idea to start off with an outline that includes the information you will put in your essay and the order in which it will be written. All rules of standard written English apply. Your paper should be typed using 10-12 size font. Your grading scale is on the back.

Writing Assignment Grading Scale

Name________________________________ Period__________ Date_________________

Grading Rubric
First Draft (20pts.) __________

Accuracy of information (20pts.) __________

Organization and clarity of information (20pts.) __________

Punctuation, grammar, spelling (20pts.) __________

Overall effort and included all required information (20pts.) __________
Total points =100

Your score __________

Comments:

____
____
____
____

Writing Assignment Grading Scale

Name________________________________ Period__________ Date_________________

Grading Rubric
First Draft (20pts.) __________

Accuracy of information (20pts.) __________

Organization and clarity of information (20pts.) __________

Punctuation, grammar, spelling (20pts.) __________

Overall effort and included all required information (20pts.) __________

Total points =100

Your score __________

Comments:

____
____
____
____

LESSON PLAN
A NEW NATION UNDER THE CONSTITUTION
IDENTIFYING MAIN IDEA(S) AND SUPPORTING DETAILS

Teacher:	Date:
Subject:	Period(s):
Title of Lesson:	State Standards:
Common Core Standards and Indicators: **RH.9-10.2.** Determine the central ideas or information of a primary or secondary source; provide an accurate summary of how key events or ideas develop over the course of the text	College Readiness Standards: **ACT-CR: Reading, ACT-CR: Score Range 16–19** **Main Ideas and Author's Approach:** Identify a clear main idea or purpose of straightforward paragraphs in uncomplicated literary narratives; **Supporting Details:** Locate simple details at the sentence and paragraph level in uncomplicated passages

Purpose/ Objective	Students will understand some of the important early events in United States history while enhancing their literacy skills through the identification of main ideas and supporting details.
Materials	Blank main idea/supporting details worksheet, answer key to main idea/supporting details worksheet, textbook
Procedures	Pass out the blank main idea/supporting details worksheet contained on the following page. Read through the items students will read about and complete the first item together as an example to the class on how to locate main ideas and supporting details. Allow students to work in pairs or groups. When all groups are done have the groups share their answers with the class. Or, turn this into a jig saw activity with each group sharing their particular topic with the class. Make a transparency out of the completed answer key located on the following pages and display to the class using an overhead projector. Let the class compare their answers to the possible answers on the key then collect and grade.
Assessment	This assignment can be graded using a standard grading scale. Students can also be quizzed or tested on items.
Comments	Stress the concept of sectionalism (loyalty to a particular part of the country) when explaining the emergence of two political parties. Completed answer key can also be used as lecture notes with students completing blank sheets while listening to the teacher explain the importance of these items.

Main Idea/Supporting Details Worksheet

Topic	Directions: Indentify the main idea(s) and 2-3 supporting details for each topic in the spaces below.
Judiciary Act of 1789	Main Idea(s): Supporting Details:
Alexander Hamilton & Thomas Jefferson	Main Idea(s): Supporting Details:
The National Bank & Hamilton's Debt Plan	Main Idea(s): Supporting Details:
Strict and Loose Construction of the Constitution	Main Idea(s): Supporting Details:
Whiskey Rebellion	Main Idea(s): Supporting Details:
Washington's Farewell Address & the election of 1796 (Federalists v. Democratic-Republicans)	Main Idea(s): Supporting Details:

Main Idea/Supporting Details Worksheet

Topic	Directions: Indentify the main idea(s) and 2-3 supporting details for each topic in the spaces below.
Judiciary Act of 1789	**Main Idea(s):** Created a federal district court for each state. **Supporting Details:** Called for six justices to be appointed by the president and approved by the Senate.
Alexander Hamilton & Thomas Jefferson	**Main Idea(s):** Hamilton was Washington's Secretary of the Treasury and oversaw the nation's finances; Jefferson was Washington's Secretary of State. **Supporting Details:** Hamilton believed in a strong central government and was influenced by the book *The Wealth of Nations*; he believed capitalism was the best type of economy for our country, and in an economy based largely on commerce and manufacturing; Jefferson believed in limiting the federal government's power and in an agrarian economy based on independent farmers.
The National Bank & Hamilton's Debt Plan	**Main Idea(s):** Hamilton wanted to create a central banking system for the country; he also believed paying off the country's Revolutionary War debt was vital to the economic health of the country. **Supporting Details:** The Bank of the United States would have branches in each major city, would provide a safe place to deposit and manage the nation's money, and could make loans to the government when necessary; Hamilton wanted to issue bonds to pay off $77 million in debts including assuming all of the debt incurred by the individual states during the Revolutionary War.
Strict and Loose Construction of the Constitution	**Main Idea(s):** Strict and loose construction refers to ways of interpreting the Constitution. **Supporting Details:** Strict interpretation limits the government's power because it only allows the government to do exactly what it is stated in the Constitution. This view was supported by Jefferson; Loose interpretation expands the government's power by allowing the government to things that are not specifically prohibited in the Constitution. Hamilton supported this view and is was how he justified the national bank plan.
Whiskey Rebellion	**Main Idea(s):** This event was the first real challenge to government authority when Pennsylvania farmers refused to pay the new Whiskey tax. The event showed the president was able to enforce the nation's laws. **Supporting Details:** Whiskey Tax passed in 1791; rebellion took place in 1794; Washington sent in 13,000 militia men to put down the rebellion.
Washington's Farewell Address & the election of 1796 (Federalists v. Democratic-Republicans)	**Main Idea(s):** Washington warned against foreign and domestic alliances in his farewell speech when he decided not to seek re-election in 1796; the competition for the presidency in 1796 election led to the rise of political parties in the country. **Supporting Details:** Washington warned against political parties but followers of Adams and Hamilton formed the Federalist Party, and followers of Thomas Jefferson formed the Democratic-Republicans. The Federalists believed in a strong central government and were supported by urban, New England manufacturers, merchants, lawyers. The Democratic-Republicans believed in state's rights and were mostly supported by rural planters, small farmers, and artisans.

LESSON PLAN
EVENTS OF THE EARLY 1800S
IDENTIFYING MAIN IDEA(S) AND SUPPORTING DETAILS

Teacher:	Date:
Subject:	Period(s):
Title of Lesson:	State Standards:
Common Core Standards and Indicators: **RH.9-10.2.** Determine the central ideas or information of a primary or secondary source; provide an accurate summary of how key events or ideas develop over the course of the text	College Readiness Standards: **ACT-CR: Reading, ACT-CR: Score Range 16–19** **Main Ideas and Author's Approach:** Identify a clear main idea or purpose of straightforward paragraphs in uncomplicated literary narratives; **Supporting Details:** Locate simple details at the sentence and paragraph level in uncomplicated passages

Purpose/ Objective	Students will understand some of the important early events in United States history while enhancing their literacy skills through the identification of main ideas and supporting details.
Materials	Blank main idea/supporting details worksheet, answer key to main idea/supporting details worksheet, textbook
Procedures	Pass out the blank main idea/supporting details worksheet contained on the following page. Read through the items students will read about and complete the first item together as an example to the class on how to locate main ideas and supporting details. Allow students to work in pairs or groups. When all groups are done have the groups share their answers with the class. Or, turn this into a jig saw activity with each group sharing their particular topic with the class. Make a transparency out of the completed answer key located on the following pages and display to the class using an overhead projector. Let the class compare their answers to the possible answers on the key. Collect and grade.
Assessment	This assignment can be graded using a standard grading scale. Students can also be quizzed or tested on items.
Comments	Be sure to explain how impressment along with other violations of American neutrality was a major cause of the War of 1812 as well as the War Hawks' desire for Canada. Explain the importance of Ft. McHenry and Battle of New Orleans. Completed answer key can also be used as lecture notes with students completing blank sheets while listening to the teacher explain the importance of these items.

Main Idea/Supporting Details Worksheet

Topic	Directions: Indentify the main idea(s) and 2-3 supporting details for each topic in the spaces below.
Election of 1800	Main Idea(s): Supporting Details:
Marbury v. Madison & Judicial Review	Main Idea(s): Supporting Details:
Louisiana Purchase	Main Idea(s): Supporting Details:
Lewis and Clark Expedition	Main Idea(s): Supporting Details:
War of 1812 &	Main Idea(s): Supporting Details:
Treaty of Ghent	Main Idea(s): Supporting Details:

Main Idea/Supporting Details Worksheet

Topic	Directions: Indentify the main idea(s) and 2-3 supporting details for each topic in the spaces below.
Election of 1800	**Main Idea(s):** Thomas Jefferson ran for president a second time and won in an election where Jefferson and Aaron Burr received the same number of electoral votes. **Supporting Details:** Hamilton didn't like Burr so he persuaded other federalists to vote for Jefferson; Jefferson became the 3rd president of the United States; the Federalist Party lost power; the election crisis prompted Congress to pass the Twelfth Amendment, which requires electors to vote for president and vice-president on separate ballots.
Marbury v. Madison & Judicial Review	**Main Idea(s):** Supreme Court case that established the precedent of Judicial Review, which is the power the of Court to declare a law unconstitutional. **Supporting Details:** Occurred in 1803 when William Marbury was not seated as a Federal judge though he was appointed by John Adams. Marbury asked the Supreme Court to force the Jefferson administration to give him his position, and the Court declared part of the Judiciary Act of 1789 unconstitutional.
Louisiana Purchase	**Main Idea(s):** Jefferson doubled the size of the United States when he purchased the Louisiana Territory from France in 1803. **Supporting Details:** Napoleon Bonaparte ruler of France; sold land for $15 million; Rocky Mountains to the Mississippi River, Canada to the Gulf of Mexico.
Lewis and Clark Expedition	**Main Idea(s):** Sent by President Jefferson in 1804 to explore and map all the land claimed in the Louisiana Purchase. **Supporting Details:** Left from St. Louis and mostly followed the Missouri River to Pacific Ocean; kept detailed records of their travels and were helped by a fur trader and his Indian wife, Sacagawea.
War of 1812 &	**Main Idea(s):** Major war fought between the U.S. and Britain from 1812 to 1814. Major causes were British violations of American neutrality rights on the high seas and British impressment of American sailors. Congressional "War Hawks" also saw opportunity to take Canada from Britain. **Supporting Details:** Washington D.C. and President's Mansion destroyed; attack on Ft. McHenry in Baltimore resulted in Francis Scott Key writing the Star Spangled Banner; Battle of New Orleans made a national hero out of Andrew Jackson.
Treaty of Ghent	**Main Idea(s):** Treaty that ended the War of 1812. War not a victory for either side but U.S. strengthened its control over the Northwest Territory and Indian resistance there was mostly eliminated. **Supporting Details:** Signed in Ghent, Belgium on December 24, 1814. Federalist party lost all remaining support after war.

LESSON PLAN
WORKING WITH A FORMAL OUTLINE
A NEW NATION UNDER THE CONSTITUTION

Teacher:	Date:
Subject:	Period(s):
Title of Lesson:	State Standards:
Common Core Standards and Indicators: **RH.11-12.2.** Determine the central ideas or information of a primary or secondary source; provide an accurate summary that makes clear the relationships among the key details and ideas	College Readiness Standards: **ACT-CR: Reading, ACT-CR: Score Range 16–19** **Main Ideas and Author's Approach:** Identify a clear main idea or purpose of straightforward paragraphs in uncomplicated literary narratives **Supporting Details:** Locate simple details at the sentence and paragraph level in uncomplicated passages

Purpose/ Objective	To provide students with an overview of major events early in the nation's history in outline form while enhancing their literacy skills in the process. This activity will target students' reading and writing skills through the identification and summarization of main ideas and supporting details.
Materials	Copies of outline notes on following pages from Washington's presidency through the War of 1812, transparency of outline notes, textbook
Procedures	Pass out copies of the outline. Highlighted areas indicate where students must complete part of the outline with information from their textbook. Put transparency of outline on overhead projector and complete a couple of the supporting details together with the class as an example. Allow students to work on outline in class for two days with teacher assistance then allow students to complete the outline for homework.
Assessment	This activity can be graded as a notebook assignment.
Comments	Teacher should decide the number of supporting details students should find. Use this outline as guide. Working with formal outlines can encompass a wide range of literacy skills depending how detailed the teacher/student wants to break down the information.

A New Nation under the Constitution

I. Washington becomes president

   A. Bills of Rights passed protecting people's basic rights

      1. Supporting details…

   B. Judiciary Act passed creating a federal court system

      1. Supporting details…

   C. Washington appoints his cabinet members

      1. Supporting details…

II. Hamilton's economic ideas are adopted creating a strong economy

   A. Hamilton influenced by Adam Smith's book

      1. Wealth of Nations
      2. More supporting details…

   B. Hamilton's plan to pay off the country's debt to restore nation's credit

      1. Supporting details…

      2. Deal with Jefferson to move the capital to Washington D.C.

   C. Hamilton's Bank proposal to help the nation manage its money

      1. What would this do? Why did people oppose this?

      2. Strict and loose construction of Constitution

      3. More supporting details…

   D. Hamilton's views were quite different than Jefferson's on the economy and government

      1. Supporting details… What did they each believe?

III. Challenges to the new government

   A. The Whiskey Rebellion was the first real challenge to federal authority

      1. Supporting details

B. Indians made settling the Northwest Territory's frontier difficult
   1. Supporting details

   2. Battle of Fallen Timbers

      a. Results and supporting details

IV. Washington does not seek re-election in 1796 setting precedent for only serving two terms

   A. Washington's Farewell address warned of potential problems
      1. Warned against political parties
      2. Warned against foreign alliance (agreements with other countries)

   B. Election of 1796 created the first political parties

      1. Federalist were led by John Adams

         a. What did they believe?

      2. Democratic-Republicans were led by Thomas Jefferson

         a. What did they believe?

      3. Who became president and vice-president?

V. Federalist Era

   A. John Adams had many problems while president that he did not handle very well

      1. XYZ affair
      2. Alien and Sedition Acts

VI. Thomas Jefferson elected president in 1800

   A. Case of *Marbury v. Madison* established power of judicial review
      1. Supporting details…
   B. Jefferson completed Louisiana Purchase, doubling the size of the country
      1. Supporting details…
   C. Jefferson sent Lewis and Clark to explore the new territory
      1. Supporting details…
   D. Importance of the Louisiana Purchase (you complete main idea and supporting details)

VII. James Madison elected president in 1808

A. The U.S. and Great Britain go to war again in the War of 1812

1. Impressment and violation of neutrality rights were main causes

2. American War Hawks saw a chance to take Canada from Britain

3. British burned Washington

4. Star Spangle Banner wrote during attack on Baltimore

5. Battle of New Orleans made hero out of Andrew Jackson

6. Treaty of Ghent ended war

a. Explain results of the war

LESSON PLAN
CAMPAIGN POSTER ACTIVITY
THE ELECTION OF 1796
THE FEDERALISTS V. THE DEMOCRATIC-REPUBLICANS

Teacher:	Date:
Subject:	Period(s):
Title of Lesson:	State Standards:
Common Core Standards and Indicators: **RH.11-12.2.** Determine the central ideas or information of a primary or secondary source; provide an accurate summary that makes clear the relationships among the key details and ideas	College Readiness Standards: **ACT-CR: Reading, ACT-CR: Score Range 16–19 Generalizations and Conclusions:** Draw simple generalizations and conclusions about people, ideas, and so on in uncomplicated passages

Purpose/ Objective	Students will understand how the emergence of political parties can be traced back to the election of 1796 when the Federalist and Democratic-Republicans competed for control of the White House and for the direction the country would take. Students will also understand the major differing beliefs the parties held about the possible social, political and economic paths the country could take (Hamiltonian v. Jeffersonian beliefs).
Materials	Textbook, Internet, colored pencils, blank paper, poster board
Procedures	Pass out project directions slips contained on following page (two sets of directions are contained on one page to save paper when copying). Students will use the information they have already learned to make posters representing the beliefs of the Federalist and Democratic-Republicans. Allow students to work in pairs or groups. Display completed posters around the room.
Assessment	Use a simple sliding scale to grade the posters or create a more detailed rubric.
Comments	This project can also be done using programs such as Microsoft Publisher.

Campaign Poster Activity

The Federalists v. The Democratic-Republicans

Despite George Washington's warnings about the dangers of political parties and forming various types of permanent alliances, foreign or domestic, the origins of political parties in the United States can be traced back to the presidential election of 1796 where followers of Thomas Jefferson (the Democratic-Republicans) and the followers of Alexander Hamilton and John Adams (the Federalists) squared off against each other.

Students will work in groups of two or four to make campaign posters for the Federalists and the Democratic-Republicans for the 1796 presidential election. The posters should illustrate the major beliefs of each party, including their views on the economy, their views on interpreting the Constitution (strict or loose), their views on the power of the federal government compared to the power of the states, and the backgrounds of their respective supporters including the geographic regions that tended to support each party. Groups may use colored pencils, markers, and paper/poster board to complete this activity or by using computer-generated presentation programs such as PowerPoint or Publisher.

Campaign Poster Activity

The Federalists v. The Democratic-Republicans

Despite George Washington's warnings about the dangers of political parties and forming various types of permanent alliances, foreign or domestic, the origins of political parties in the United States can be traced back to the presidential election of 1796 where followers of Thomas Jefferson (the Democratic-Republicans) and the followers of Alexander Hamilton and John Adams (the Federalists) squared off against each other.

Students will work in groups of two or four to make campaign posters for the Federalists and the Democratic-Republicans for the 1796 presidential election. The posters should illustrate the major beliefs of each party, including their views on the economy, their views on interpreting the Constitution (strict or loose), their views on the power of the federal government compared to the power of the states, and the backgrounds of their respective supporters including the geographic regions that tended to support each party. Groups may use colored pencils, markers, and paper/poster board to complete this activity or by using computer-generated presentation programs such as PowerPoint or Publisher.

LESSON PLAN
WEB DIAGRAM AND SUMMARY
A NEW NATION UNDER THE CONSTITUTION

Teacher:	Date:
Subject:	Period(s):
Title of Lesson:	State Standards:
Common Core Standards and Indicators: **RH.11-12.2.** Determine the central ideas or information of a primary or secondary source; provide an accurate summary that makes clear the relationships among the key details and ideas	College Readiness Standards: **ACT-CR: Reading, ACT-CR: Score Range 24–27** **Main Ideas and Author's Approach:** Summarize basic events and ideas in more challenging passages

Purpose/ Objective	To help students understand, review, and summarize some of the important events early in the nation's history.
Materials	White board and markers or chalkboard, student notes, and assignments on related topics
Procedures	Teacher will lead the class in a review of important events early in the nation's history. Students will guide the teacher in completing the web diagram. Draw a circle in the center of the board and in the circle write "A New Nation Under the Constitution." Ask students to recall some of the important events they have recently learned about the first few presidencies. Important events such the Judiciary Act of 1789 or the Election of 1796 should be organized in other circles as main ideas in the creation of a web diagram that further explains the main topic. Use the diagram on the next page as a guide. Ask students to recall specific supporting details about each main idea and write them next to the circles, like spokes coming off the hub of a bicycle tire (examples of possible supporting details are listed below the sample web diagram on the following page).
Assessment	Ask students to write a summary of the events using the web diagram as a guide. Tell students they should simply use the main ideas and supporting details in the diagram to reconstruct the information in paragraph form.
Comments	This technique of using a web diagram to explain and summarize events and concepts can be beneficial to students with low reading abilities as well as special education students, both of whom often benefit from more graphic representations of information. This same technique can be used for the other web diagram activities in this book.

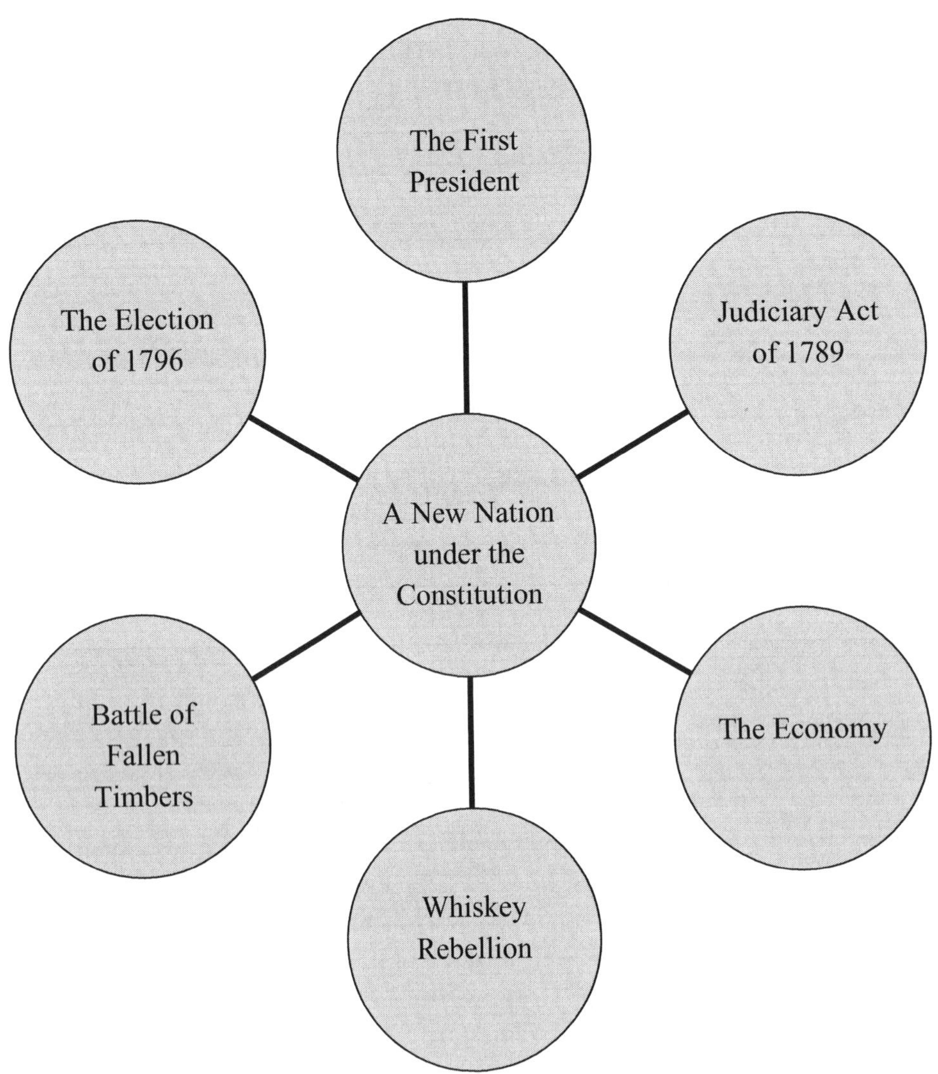

The First President
George Washington
John Adams (vice-president)
Thomas Jefferson (Sec. of State)
Alexander Hamilton (Sec. of Treasury)

The Judiciary Act of 1789
Established federal courts

The Battle of Fallen Timbers
Cleared N.W. Territory of Indian Resistance
Took place in present-day Ohio in 1794

Whiskey Rebellion
First challenge to federal authority
Pennsylvania, 1794
Farmers didn't want to pay tax
Washington sent in troops

The Economy
Alexander Hamilton
Capitalism
Debt Plan
National Bank
Strict v. Loose interpretation of Constitution
Deal to move capital of country to Washington D.C.

Election of 1796
Gave rise to political parties
Federalists v. Democratic-Republicans
Adams defeated Jefferson

Name______________________________

Short-Answer Test

A New Nation Under the Constitution

1. Name the first two presidents of the United States.

2. What was the Judiciary Act of 1789?

3. Explain what the Bank of the United States was and why Hamilton was in favor of a national bank and why Jefferson was not. Whose view won out and why?

4. Explain Loose v. Strict interpretation of the Constitution. Who supported each view?

5. What was the Whiskey Rebellion and why was it important?

6. Where was the first capital of the United States and why was Washington D.C. finally chosen to be the nation's permanent capital?

7. What did George Washington warn against in his farewell speech?

8. Explain how political parties developed in this country. What were the first two political parties and what did they stand for? Explain the difference between a Hamiltonian America v. a Jeffersonian America.

9. Explain the Alien and Sedition Acts. Why were they passed and who were they aimed at? What constitutional issues did they bring up?

10. Who were the "Midnight Judges" and what effect did they have on the federal court system?

LESSON PLAN
OPPOSING VIEWS
WRITING ASSIGNMENT ON THE NATIONAL BANK

Teacher:	Date:
Subject:	Period(s):
Title of Lesson:	State Standards:
Common Core Standards and Indicators: **RH.11-12.6.** Evaluate authors' differing points of view on the same historical event or issue by assessing the authors' claims, reasoning, and evidence. **WHST.11-12.1b.** Develop claim(s) and counterclaims fairly and thoroughly, supplying the most relevant data and evidence for each while pointing out the strengths and limitations of both claim(s) and counterclaims in a discipline-appropriate form that anticipates the audience's knowledge level, concerns, values, and possible biases	College Readiness Standards: **ACT-CR: Reading, ACT-CR: Score Range 20–23** **Generalizations and Conclusions:** Draw simple generalizations and conclusions using details that support the main points of more challenging passages

Purpose/ Objective	Students will learn more about the decision by President Washington to support the chartering of a national bank and be given an opportunity to express their opinions on this issue, both pro and con, while enhancing their reading and writing skills.
Materials	Assignment directions and grading scale, pro and con articles on the national bank from *Opposing Views in American History, Volume I*
Procedures	Copy and pass out assignment directions and assignment grading scale (two assignment directions and two simple grading rubrics are contained on separate pages to save paper). Explain directions to students. Start of by asking students why banks are important today and the purpose(s) they serve. Ask them to imagine a country with no banks then begin to explain that the decision to create a national banking system was extremely controversial. Include the differing opinions of Jefferson and Hamilton on this issue as well as their views on strict and loose interpretation of the Constitution. Allow students ample class time to work on this so teacher can help them both with the writing and the reading of materials.
Assessment	Use the grading rubric included with this activity or teacher can design a new one.
Comments	The articles in *Opposing Views in American History, Volume I*, by William Dudley and published by Greenhaven Press were used for this assignment.

Writing Assignment
Opposing Views in American History: The National Bank

Imagine our world today without banks. Where would the people of our country deposit their money? Where people go to borrow money? How would the government keep track of all the money in circulation? The decision to create a national banking system for the United States was actually a very controversial decision that not everyone supported. This topic forced the leaders of our young country to take sides on the issue. The two main questions were whether or not the Constitution gave the government the power to create a national bank and whether or not it was actually necessary and good for the country. Alexander Hamilton was a major supporter of the national bank, and Thomas Jefferson was against the national bank. Our first president, George Washington, eventually listened to Hamilton and created a national banking system.

Your assignment is to read the pages in your textbook and the handouts about the national banking system and write an essay that summarizes both sides of the argument. Your introduction should explain when the banking system was created and why it has been important. In the body of your essay you should summarize the opposing views about creating a national bank. **Make sure you explain the major reasons for and against creating a national banking system.** In your conclusion briefly restate the main points you have made in the essay and which side of the argument makes more sense. Which view do you agree with and why? Before you start writing be sure to make an outline of the main points you will include in your essay. Your grading scale is on the back.

Writing Assignment
Opposing Views in American History: The National Bank

Imagine our world today without banks. Where would the people of our country deposit their money? Where people go to borrow money? How would the government keep track of all the money in circulation? The decision to create a national banking system for the United States was actually a very controversial decision that not everyone supported. This topic forced the leaders of our young country to take sides on the issue. The two main questions were whether or not the Constitution gave the government the power to create a national bank and whether or not it was actually necessary and good for the country. Alexander Hamilton was a major supporter of the national bank, and Thomas Jefferson was against the national bank. Our first president, George Washington, eventually listened to Hamilton and created a national banking system.

Your assignment is to read the pages in your textbook and the handouts about the national banking system and write an essay that summarizes both sides of the argument. Your introduction should explain when the banking system was created and why it has been important. In the body of your essay you should summarize the opposing views about creating a national bank. **Make sure you explain the major reasons for and against creating a national banking system.** In your conclusion briefly restate the main points you have made in the essay and which side of the argument makes more sense. Which view do you agree with and why? Before you start writing be sure to make an outline of the main points you will include in your essay. Your grading scale is on the back.

Writing Assignment Grading Scale

Name________________________________ Period__________ Date_________________

Grading Rubric
First Draft (20pts.) __________

Accuracy of information (20pts.) __________

Organization and clarity of information (20pts.) __________

Punctuation, grammar, spelling (20pts.) __________

Overall effort and included all required information (20pts.) __________
Total points =100

Your score __________

Comments:
____
____
____
____

Writing Assignment Grading Scale

Name________________________________ Period__________ Date_________________

Grading Rubric
First Draft (20pts.) __________

Accuracy of information (20pts.) __________

Organization and clarity of information (20pts.) __________

Punctuation, grammar, spelling (20pts.) __________

Overall effort and included all required information (20pts.) __________

Total points =100

Your score __________

Comments:
____
____
____
____

LESSON PLAN
THE LOUISIANA PURCHASE AND EARLY WESTWARD EXPANSION MAP

Teacher:	Date:
Subject:	Period(s):
Title of Lesson:	State Standards:
Common Core Standards and Indicators: **RH.11-12.7.** Integrate and evaluate multiple sources of information presented in diverse formats and media (e.g., visually, quantitatively, as well as in words) in order to address a question or solve a problem.	College Readiness Standards: **ACT-CR: Reading, ACT-CR: Score Range 16–19** **Generalizations and Conclusions:** Draw simple generalizations and conclusions about people, ideas, and so on in uncomplicated passages

Purpose/ Objective	Students will strengthen their geography and map reading skills while learning more about early westward expansion.
Materials	Assignment directions from next page, colored pencils, textbook, blank outline map of the United States or the Louisiana Territory
Procedures	Pass out copies of the map directions contained on the following page. Allow students to work on map activity in class for a day or two and complete the rest for homework.
Assessment	This assignment can be graded by creating a rubric or simply grading it on a sliding scale. Teacher will determine the point value of the assignment. Points are subtracted for every item missing.
Comments	Two sets of directions are contained on one page to save paper. Copy directions and cut into slips. More points should be subtracted for the more important or more time consuming items required for the assignment.

The Louisiana Purchase and Early Westward Expansion Map

Using various maps in your textbook or from the Internet, you are to create a map showing the progress of early western settlement and expansion in the United States. Use different colors to designate the United States before 1803 (before the Louisiana Territory was purchased), the part of the United States that was called the Northwest Territory (not Indiana Territory) and the Louisiana Purchase Territory itself. Label all the states at the time including the states that comprised the Northwest Territory. Label the land that still belonged to Spain at this time.

Be sure to include such items as the Rocky Mountains; the Appalachian Mountains; the Cumberland Gap; the Battle of Fallen Timbers; the Lewis and Clark Expedition (trace their route on the map); the Great Lakes; and the Mississippi, Missouri, Ohio, Columbia and Snake rivers. Use different colors for each item and don't forget to make a map key. Remember, interpreting maps is a skill. Do not simply copy the maps exactly as you might see them in the book. Construct your own map and only include information you have been asked to include.

The Louisiana Purchase and Early Westward Expansion Map

Using various maps in your textbook or from the Internet, you are to create a map showing the progress of early western settlement and expansion in the United States. Use different colors to designate the United States before 1803 (before the Louisiana Territory was purchased), the part of the United States that was called the Northwest Territory (not Indiana Territory) and the Louisiana Purchase Territory itself. Label all the states at the time including the states that comprised the Northwest Territory. Label the land that still belonged to Spain at this time.

Be sure to include such items as the Rocky Mountains; the Appalachian Mountains; the Cumberland Gap; the Battle of Fallen Timbers; the Lewis and Clark Expedition (trace their route on the map); the Great Lakes; and the Mississippi, Missouri, Ohio, Columbia, and Snake rivers. Use different colors for each item and don't forget to make a map key. Remember, interpreting maps is a skill. Do not simply copy the maps exactly as you might see them in the book. Construct your own map and only include information you have been asked to include.

LESSON PLAN
ECONOMIC AND POLITICAL DEVELOPMENTS IN THE UNITED STATES AFTER THE WAR OF 1812
IDENTIFYING MAIN IDEA(S) AND SUPPORTING DETAILS

Teacher:	Date:
Subject:	Period(s):
Title of Lesson:	State Standards:
Common Core Standards and Indicators: **RH.9-10.2.** Determine the central ideas or information of a primary or secondary source; provide an accurate summary of how key events or ideas develop over the course of the text	College Readiness Standards: **ACT-CR: Reading, ACT-CR: Score Range 16–19** **Main Ideas and Author's Approach:** Identify a clear main idea or purpose of straightforward paragraphs in uncomplicated literary narratives **Supporting Details:** Locate simple details at the sentence and paragraph level in uncomplicated passages

Purpose/ Objective	Students will understand some of the important early events in United States history while enhancing their literacy skills through the identification of main ideas and supporting details.
Materials	Blank main idea/supporting details worksheet, answer key to main idea/supporting details worksheet, textbook
Procedures	Pass out the blank main idea/supporting details worksheet contained on the following page. Read through the items students will read about and complete the first item together as an example to the class on how to locate main ideas and supporting details. Allow students to work in pairs or groups. When all groups are done have the groups share their answers with the class. Or, turn this into a jig saw activity with each group sharing their particular topic with the class. Make a transparency out of the completed answer key located on the following pages and display to class using an overhead projector. Let the class compare their answers to the possible answers on the key. Collect and grade.
Assessment	This assignment can be graded using a standard grading scale. Students can also be quizzed or tested on items.
Comments	Completed answer key can also be used as lecture notes with students completing blank sheets while listening to the teacher explain the importance of these items.

Main Idea/Supporting Details Worksheet

Topic	**Directions: Indentify the main idea(s) and 2-3 supporting details for each topic in the spaces below.**
American System	Main Idea(s): Supporting Details:
Market Revolution	Main Idea(s): Supporting Details:
1st Industrial Revolution	Main Idea(s): Supporting Details:
Missouri Compromise	Main Idea(s): Supporting Details:
Monroe Doctrine	Main Idea(s): Supporting Details:
Election of 1824	Main Idea(s): Supporting Details:

Main Idea/Supporting Details Worksheet

Topic	Directions: Indentify the main idea(s) and 2-3 supporting details for each topic in the spaces below.
American System	**Main Idea(s):** Henry Clay's idea to increase federal involvement in the economy after the War of 1812. **Supporting Details:** Three parts…a national bank; a protective tariff to encourage industrial manufacturing; a national transportation system to facilitate the movement of people and goods.
Market Revolution	**Main Idea(s):** The manufacturing of goods that were sold all over the country rather than items just being made and sold in small regions. **Supporting Details:** Made possible by the new roads, canals and railroads that made it possible to link various parts of the country together and transport products quickly. Changed the economy and the way people did business. Regions no longer had to be self-sufficient
1st Industrial Revolution	**Main Idea(s):** A shift from the local hand-production of goods to the manufacturing of goods in large quantities by machines in factories (mass production). **Supporting Details:** Early industrialization took place in the textile industry in the U.S. in the late 1700s then spread to other industries. Eli Whitney's concept of interchangeable parts was applied to manufacturing of other products.
Missouri Compromise	**Main Idea(s):** Henry Clay's plan in 1820 to preserve the balance of power between slave and free states and solve the debate over where slavery should be allowed to exist when Missouri applied for statehood in 1819. **Supporting Details:** Missouri became a slave state, Maine admitted as free state, and an imaginary line drawn through Louisiana Territory at 36°30'. Slavery was to be outlawed above this line.
Monroe Doctrine	**Main Idea(s):** President Monroe's statement in his annual message to Congress in which he warned European countries not to interfere with the newly-immerging, independent countries in Latin America or try to establish new colonies in the Western Hemisphere. **Supporting Details:** December 23, 1823. Became part of American foreign policy.
Election of 1824	**Main Idea(s):** John Quincy Adams (son of John Adams) defeated war hero Andrew Jackson in the 1824 presidential election. **Supporting Details:** Jackson won the popular vote, but no candidate won a majority of electoral votes. House of Representative chose John Quincy Adams to become president. Henry Clay urged his supporters in the House to choose Adams over Jackson, and when Adams became president Clay was named Secretary of State. Jackson and his supporters claimed a "corrupt bargain" had been struck.

LESSON PLAN
TURNING AN OUTLINE INTO AN ESSAY
POLITICAL AND ECONOMIC DEVELOPMENTS AFTER THE WAR OF 1812

Teacher:	Date:
Subject:	Period(s):
Title of Lesson:	State Standards:
Common Core Standards and Indicators: **WHST.9-10.4.** Produce clear and coherent writing in which the development, organization, and style are appropriate to task, purpose, and audience.	College Readiness Standards: **ACT-CR: Reading, ACT-CR: Score Range 20–23 Generalizations and Conclusions:** Draw simple generalizations and conclusions using details that support the main points of more challenging passages

Purpose/ Objective	Students will improve their literacy skills by learning how to turn a formal outline into an essay using main ideas while summarizing events in United States' history after the War of 1812.
Materials	Handout on next page on turning an outline into an essay and handout on transition words if desired by teacher
Procedures	Have students use the Main Idea/Supporting Details worksheet they just completed as a guide to outline the pages in their textbook (just like before…organizing information in the outline into main ideas and supporting details) about the various economic and political developments in the United States after the War of 1812. Copy and pass out the handout on the next page on turning an outline into an essay as a guide for students. Go over handout with students. Have students use the outline to write a multi-paragraph summary about those developments. The outline should contain the items on the Main Idea/Supporting Detail sheet. If desired, create and provide students with a handout or list of transition words such as *however, despite, regardless, for example, therefore, first, likewise, another, hence, furthermore*, etc. that helps students connect ideas and paragraphs.
Assessment	Grade the summary essay using a standard grading scale.
Comments	It can be extremely useful to give students writing prompts to help get students started. Give examples and have students come up with their own examples of prompts for the class. Tell students they can choose one. Note: the history book used for this example is *American Nation* by Paul Boyer and published by Holt, Rinehart and Winston; copyright 2007.

Turning an Outline into an Essay Using Main Ideas to Create Paragraphs

Sample Outline:

I Growth and Challenges

A) The Economy

1. The War of 1812 forced Americans to produce more goods themselves
2. Many people began to understand the nation had to balance agriculture, commerce and manufacturing
3. The war revealed the weaknesses in the nation's financial system
   a. The nation needed a strong national bank
4. The war also revealed the nation's transportation problems

B) The American System

1. Henry Clay's idea for the nation after the War of 1812
2. Called for federal involvement in the economy
   a. stronger national bank
   b. protective tariffs
   c. a national transportation system

Topic Sentence for First Paragraph (1st main idea): *The War of 1812 revealed many problems in nation's economic and financial systems.* Many people began to believe the nation had to balance the needs of agriculture, commerce and manufacturing.

Connect Paragraphs and Thoughts Using Transition Words: However, despite, regardless, for example, therefore, first, likewise, another, hence, furthermore, etc.

Topic Sentence for Second Paragraph (2nd main idea) Topic Sentence: *Therefore, the American System was proposed by Henry Clay, which called for more federal involvement in the economy.* The American System had three main aspects.

Essay Writing Prompt: "After the War of 1812, the nation faced several new challenges but eventually experienced rapid growth in the economy and manufacturing."

LESSON PLAN
ANDREW JACKSON
IDENTIFYING MAIN IDEA(S) AND SUPPORTING DETAILS

Teacher:	Date:
Subject:	Period(s):
Title of Lesson:	State Standards:
Common Core Standards and Indicators: **RH.9-10.2.** Determine the central ideas or information of a primary or secondary source; provide an accurate summary of how key events or ideas develop over the course of the text	College Readiness Standards: **ACT-CR: Reading, ACT-CR: Score Range 16–19** **Main Ideas and Author's Approach:** Identify a clear main idea or purpose of straightforward paragraphs in uncomplicated literary narratives **Supporting Details:** Locate simple details at the sentence and paragraph level in uncomplicated passages

Purpose/ Objective	Students will understand some of the important events and aspects of Andrew Jackson's presidency while enhancing their literacy skills through the identification of main ideas and supporting details.
Materials	Blank main idea/supporting details worksheet, answer key to main idea/supporting details worksheet, textbook
Procedures	Pass out the blank main idea/supporting details worksheet contained on the following page. Read through the items students will read about and complete the first item together as an example to the class on how to locate main ideas and supporting details. Allow students to work in pairs or groups. When all groups are done have the groups share their answers with the class. Or, turn this into a jig saw activity with each group sharing their particular topic with the class. Make a transparency out of the completed answer key located on the following pages and display to class using an overhead projector. Let the class compare their answers to the possible answers on the key. Collect and grade.
Assessment	This assignment can be graded using a standard grading scale. Students can also be quizzed or tested on items.
Comments	Completed answer key can also be used as lecture notes with students completing blank sheets while listening to the teacher explain the importance of these items.

Main Idea/Supporting Details Worksheet

Topic	Directions: Indentify the main idea(s) and 2-3 supporting details for each topic in the spaces below.
Election of 1828 and Jacksonian Democracy	Main Idea(s): Supporting Details:
Nullification Crisis of 1828	Main Idea(s): Supporting Details:
Indian Removal Act & Worcester v. Georgia	Main Idea(s): Supporting Details:
Trail of Tears	Main Idea(s): Supporting Details:
Panic of 1837	Main Idea(s): Supporting Details:
Whig Party	Main Idea(s): Supporting Details:

Main Idea/Supporting Details Worksheet

Topic	Directions: Indentify the main idea(s) and 2-3 supporting details for each topic in the spaces below.
Election of 1828 and Jacksonian Democracy	**Main Idea(s):** Andrew Jackson defeated John Quincy Adams in the 1828 presidential election. **Supporting Details:** Jackson and his supporters called themselves the Democratic Party. Portrayed himself as the "common man" and a "self-made" man. First modern campaign. Ushered in changes like the spoils system and rotation in office. Democratic process brought to more people at this time through greater economic opportunity as a result of the Market Revolution and expansion of voting rights through states dropping property requirements for voting and holding office. Public schools expanded...all aspects of Jacksonian Democracy.
Nullification Crisis of 1828	**Main Idea(s):** South Carolina threatened to secede in 1832 after Congress passed protective tariffs in 1828 and 1832 to protect American manufacturing. **Supporting Details:** Led by John C. Calhoun, South Carolina believed a state had the right to nullify an act of Congress it considered unconstitutional. Jackson warned against defying the laws of the country. South Carolina accepted a compromise tariff 1833.
Indian Removal Act & Worcester v. Georgia	**Main Idea(s):** Jackson ordered the removal of all remaining Indians east of the Mississippi River to Indian Territory west of the Mississippi River to clear land for agricultural production. The Cherokee Indians appealed their case to stay on their land to the Supreme Court. **Supporting Details:** Indian Removal Act passed in 1830. Supreme Court sided with the Cherokee, but Andrew Jackson disobeyed the Court and continued with removal.
Trail of Tears	**Main Idea(s):** Refers to the forced march of 16,000 Cherokee Indians from their lands to Indian Territory as part of the Indian Removal Act. **Supporting Details:** About 4,000 Indians died on this journey by 1838.
Panic of 1837	**Main Idea(s):** Refers to the financial crisis of 1837 resulting from Jackson's refusal to re-charter the national bank. **Supporting Details:** Jackson did not believe the national bank was good for the country and only benefited wealthy people at the expense of the poor and common people. Jacksons' Pet Banks issued too much money and caused wide-spread inflation causing a financial crisis.
Whig Party	**Main Idea(s):** Opponents of Andrew Jackson formed a new political party in 1834 called the Whig Party. **Supporting Details:** Whig Party took its name from the Whig Party in Britain that had opposed the king. Opponents of Andrew Jackson nicknamed him "King Andrew" because of his abuse of federal power.

LESSON PLAN
OPPOSING VIEWS
WRITING ASSIGNMENT ON VOTING RIGHTS

Teacher:	Date:
Subject:	Period(s):
Title of Lesson:	State Standards:
Common Core Standards and Indicators: **RH.11-12.6.** Evaluate authors' differing points of view on the same historical event or issue by assessing the authors' claims, reasoning, and evidence. **WHST.11-12.1b.** Develop claim(s) and counterclaims fairly and thoroughly, supplying the most relevant data and evidence for each while pointing out the strengths and limitations of both claim(s) and counterclaims in a discipline-appropriate form that anticipates the audience's knowledge level, concerns, values, and possible biases	College Readiness Standards: **ACT-CR: Reading, ACT-CR: Score Range 20–23 Generalizations and Conclusions:** Draw simple generalizations and conclusions using details that support the main points of more challenging passages

Purpose/ Objective	Students will learn more about the decision to limit voting rights to white male landowners early in country's history and be given an opportunity to express their opinions on this issue, both pro and con, while enhancing their reading and writing skills.
Materials	Assignment directions and grading scale, pro and con articles on suffrage rights from *Opposing Views in American History, Volume I*
Procedures	Copy and pass out assignment directions and assignment grading scale (two assignment directions and two simple grading rubrics are contained on separate pages to save paper). Explain directions to students. Start off with an overview of suffrage rights and how they were once restricted to white, male landowners. Explain why this happened and include the differing opinions of Jefferson and Hamilton as to whom should hold political power. Allow students ample class to time to work on this so teacher can help them both with the writing and the reading of materials.
Assessment	Use the grading rubric included with this activity or teacher can design a new one.
Comments	The articles in *Opposing Views in American History, Volume I*, by William Dudley and published by Greenhaven Press were used for this assignment.

Writing Assignment:
Opposing Views in American History

You are to read the handout that explains the different viewpoints on suffrage rights (voting rights) that existed when the United States was still a very young country. The fight over suffrage for different groups of people, particularly African Americans and women, continued for many years into our country's future, but initially, the right to vote was only given to white, male landowners. Some people were in favor of this; others thought the property ownership restriction should be removed. You are to write an essay in which you summarize the different points of view regarding early suffrage rights. **First,** start your essay off with an introduction that briefly explains the restrictions put on voting for different groups of people. **Second,** in the body of the essay, summarize the different viewpoints on suffrage rights as explained in the handouts. **Be sure to include the major reasons given to support each side. In your conclusion,** restate the two opposing viewpoints and explain which view had the best argument. Explain which view you agree with and why, as well as how voting restrictions placed on various people were in opposition to our country's founding ideas of democracy and equality. Before writing it is a good idea to start off with an outline that includes the information you will put in your essay and the order in which it will be written. All rules of standard written English apply. Your paper should be typed using 10-12 size font. Your grading scale is on the back.

Writing Assignment:
Opposing Views in American History

You are to read the handout that explains the different viewpoints on suffrage rights (voting rights) that existed when the United States was still a very young country. The fight over suffrage for different groups of people, particularly African Americans and women, continued for many years into our country's future, but initially, the right to vote was only given to white, male landowners. Some people were in favor of this; others thought the property ownership restriction should be removed. You are to write an essay in which you summarize the different points of view regarding early suffrage rights. **First,** start your essay off with an introduction that briefly explains the restrictions put on voting for different groups of people. **Second,** in the body of the essay, summarize the different viewpoints on suffrage rights as explained in the handouts. **Be sure to include the major reasons given to support each side. In your conclusion,** restate the two opposing viewpoints and explain which view had the best argument. Explain which view you agree with and why, as well as how voting restrictions placed on various people were in opposition to our country's founding ideas of democracy and equality. Before writing it is a good idea to start off with an outline that includes the information you will put in your essay and the order in which it will be written. All rules of standard written English apply. Your paper should be typed using 10-12 size font. Your grading scale is on the back.

Writing Assignment Grading Scale

Name________________________________ Period__________ Date_________________

Grading Rubric
First Draft (20pts.) __________

Accuracy of information (20pts.) __________

Organization and clarity of information (20pts.) __________

Punctuation, grammar, spelling (20pts.) __________

Overall effort and included all required information (20pts.) __________
Total points =100

Your score __________

Comments:
____
____
____
____

Writing Assignment Grading Scale

Name________________________________ Period__________ Date_________________

Grading Rubric
First Draft (20pts.) __________

Accuracy of information (20pts.) __________

Organization and clarity of information (20pts.) __________

Punctuation, grammar, spelling (20pts.) __________

Overall effort and included all required information (20pts.) __________

Total points =100

Your score __________

Comments:
____
____
____
____

Summary of Westward Expansion

When the U.S. won its independence in 1783 its boundaries stretched to the Mississippi River. Several battles with Indians cleared the land between the Appalachian Mountains and the Mississippi River for American settlement. Thomas Jefferson bought the Louisiana Territory from France in 1803, extending the country's boundaries to the Rocky Mountains. Eli Whitney's cotton gin revived the institution of slavery by creating more demand for cotton, which was an industry based on southern slave labor. As new territories became open for settlement the issue of slavery arose. Would slavery be legal there or not?

The Missouri Compromise, written by Henry Clay and adopted in 1820, tried to answer this debate once and for all. Maine was admitted as a free state, Missouri as a slave state, and an imaginary line was drawn across the Louisiana Territory. Slavery would be allowed south of the line but not north of it. About the same time, the United States bought a large portion of Florida from Spain in 1819 for $5 million in the Adams-Onis Treaty. During the early 1800s many Latin American countries won their independence from European countries such as Spain and Portugal. In an effort to keep European countries from dominating these newly independent countries or seeking new colonies, President James Monroe issued the Monroe Doctrine in 1823, a statement warning European countries to stay out of the Western Hemisphere.

Under pressure from American settlers President Andrew Jackson signed the Indian Removal Act in 1830. This forced all remaining Indians tribes living east of the Mississippi River to relocate to Indian Territory west of the Mississippi. The Cherokee Indians actually won a court case, Worchester v. Georgia, allowing them to stay on their lands. Andrew Jackson said since this was the Supreme Court's decision they should enforce the decision themselves, and he ordered the relocation anyway. This resulted in the Trails of Tears in which 16,000 Cherokees marched from Georgia to Indian Territory in the winter.

As a new spirit of nationalism swept the country in decades after the War of 1812 a new idea about land and territorial expansion became popular in the 1830s and 1840s. Manifest Destiny, a term coined in 1845 in an article about Texas annexation, by John O'Sullivan, was a belief the United States had the best form of government, economy, and society and was destined to expand coast to coast. This idea would justify the taking of land from other people.

After Mexico won its independence from Spain in 1821 it controlled the land of the American Southwest. Mexico at first encouraged Americans to move into Mexican Texas to farm the land. Many slaveholders moved into Texas as well. Soon there were more Americans in Texas than Mexicans. A battle for Texas took place resulting in the slaughtering of hundreds of Americans at the Alamo in 1836. Sam Houston captured the Mexican President, Santa Anna, and forced him to surrender Texas in 1836. Texas became an independent republic for nine years but was annexed by the U.S. in 1845, outraging Mexico. Further boundary disputes in Texas between the U.S. and Mexico and the desire for more land led to the Mexican-American War (1846-1848). Mexico was defeated and forced to sign the Treaty of Guadalupe Hidalgo, which forced Mexico to give up all its land in the American southwest (Mexican Cession). A treaty with Britain gave the U.S. control over the Oregon Country up to the 49th parallel, and in 1848, gold was discovered in near San Francisco, which brought thousands of people to California. The U.S. wanted another strip of land south of Arizona that connected to California for a rail line, so the U.S. bought that land from Mexico for $10 million in the Gadsden Purchase (1853).

Manifest Destiny and Westward Expansion Study Guide

1. Explain Manifest Destiny and how it was used to justify the taking of land.
2. What country got its independence from Spain in 1821?
3. After 1821, what country owned the land that made up Texas and the American Southwest?
4. Why did the Mexican government become upset with Americans moving into Texas?
5. Who were Stephen Austin, Sam Houston, and General Santa Anna?
6. What happened at the Alamo (1836) and how did this influence other Americans?
7. When was Texas annexed to the United States and become a state?
8. When and how did the Mexican-American War start?
9. Who was President when the war started? Do you think this President wanted a war?
10. Who were Zachary Taylor and Winfield Scott?
11. Explain the Treaty of Guadalupe Hidalgo and the Mexican Cession. What states were eventually created from this new territory?
12. What was the Gadsden Purchase? How much did it cost and why did the U.S. want it?
13. Who were mountain men and what did they do?
14. What were the Oregon, Santa Fe, and Mormon Trails?
15. Who settled Salt Lake City and why?
16. What happened to the Donner Party?
17. Whose campaign slogan was "Fifty-four forty or fight?" What did this mean?
18. What country did the U.S. make a treaty with to divide up the Oregon Territory? What was the final boundary that was agreed upon?
19. What event sped up the settlement of California?
20. What issue kept many Northern people from wanting Texas and California from becoming states right away?

LESSON PLAN
MANIFEST DESTINY MAP ASSIGNMENT

Teacher:		Date:
Subject:		Period(s):
Title of Lesson:		State Standards:
Common Core Standards and Indicators: **RH.11-12.7.** Integrate and evaluate multiple sources of information presented in diverse formats and media (e.g., visually, quantitatively, as well as in words) in order to address a question or solve a problem.		College Readiness Standards: **ACT-CR: Reading, ACT-CR: Score Range 16–19 Generalizations and Conclusions:** Draw simple generalizations and conclusions about people, ideas, and so on in uncomplicated passages
Purpose/ Objective	Students will strengthen their geography and map reading skills while learning more about the various aspects of Manifest Destiny and westward expansion.	
Materials	Assignment directions from next page, colored pencils, textbook, blank outline map of the United States	
Procedures	Pass out copies of the map directions contained on the following page. Allow students to work on map activity in class for a day or two and complete the rest for homework.	
Assessment	This assignment can be graded by creating a rubric or simply grading it on a sliding scale. Teacher will determine the point value of the assignment. Points are subtracted for every item missing.	
Comments	Two sets of directions are contained on one page to save paper. Copy directions and cut into slips. More points should be subtracted for the more important or more time-consuming items required for the assignment.	

Manifest Destiny Map Assignment

You are to make a map illustrating the concept of Manifest Destiny and aspects of the resulting territorial expansion that occurred in the mid 1800s. Label and shade each of the following in different colors and be sure to include a date for each item on the map. Include a map key as well.

1. The Alamo
2. Texas annexation
3. Rio Grande River
4. Nueces River
5. Mexican Cession
6. Oregon, Mormon, California, and Santa Fe trails
7. Oregon Country
8. Gadsden Purchase
9. Gold discovery at Sutter's Mill
10. Cities of San Antonio, Santa Fe, Salt Lake City, San Francisco

Manifest Destiny Map Assignment

You are to make a map illustrating the concept of Manifest Destiny and aspects of the resulting territorial expansion that occurred in the mid 1800s. Label and shade each of the following in different colors and be sure to include a date for each item on the map. Include a map key as well.

1. The Alamo
2. Texas annexation
3. Rio Grande River
4. Nueces River
5. Mexican Cession
6. Oregon, Mormon, California, and Santa Fe trails
7. Oregon Country
8. Gadsden Purchase
9. Gold discovery at Sutter's Mill
10. Cities of San Antonio, Santa Fe, Salt Lake City, San Francisco

LESSON PLAN
MANIFEST DESTINY WEB DIAGRAM AND SUMMARY

Teacher:	Date:
Subject:	Period(s):
Title of Lesson:	State Standards:
Common Core Standards and Indicators: **RH.11-12.2.** Determine the central ideas or information of a primary or secondary source; provide an accurate summary that makes clear the relationships among the key details and ideas	College Readiness Standards: **ACT-CR: Reading, ACT-CR: Score Range 24–27** **Main Ideas and Author's Approach:** Summarize basic events and ideas in more challenging passages

Purpose/ Objective	To help students understand, review, and summarize the concept of Manifest Destiny and its correlation to the westward expansion of the United States in the 1830s through the 1850s.
Materials	White board and markers or chalkboard, student notes, and assignments on related topics
Procedures	Teacher will lead the class in a review of important aspects of westward expansion. Students will guide the teacher in completing the web diagram. As a prompt, have students review John Gast's famous 1879 image of the spirit of manifest destiny in their textbook (or put image on overhead) to help students start making connections. Draw a circle in the center of the board and in the circle write "Manifest Destiny." Ask students to recall some of the important events they have recently learned about Manifest Destiny and westward expansion. Important events should be organized in other circles as main ideas in the creation of a web diagram that further explains the main topic. Use the diagram on the next page as a guide. Ask students to recall specific supporting details about each main idea and write them next to the circles, like spokes coming off the hub of a bicycle tire.
Assessment	Ask students to write a summary of Manifest Destiny using the web diagram as a guide. Tell students they should simply use the main ideas and supporting details in the diagram to reconstruct the information in paragraph form.
Comments	This same technique of using a web diagram to explain and summarize events and concepts can be very beneficial to students will low reading abilities as well as special education students, both of whom often benefit from more graphic representations of information.

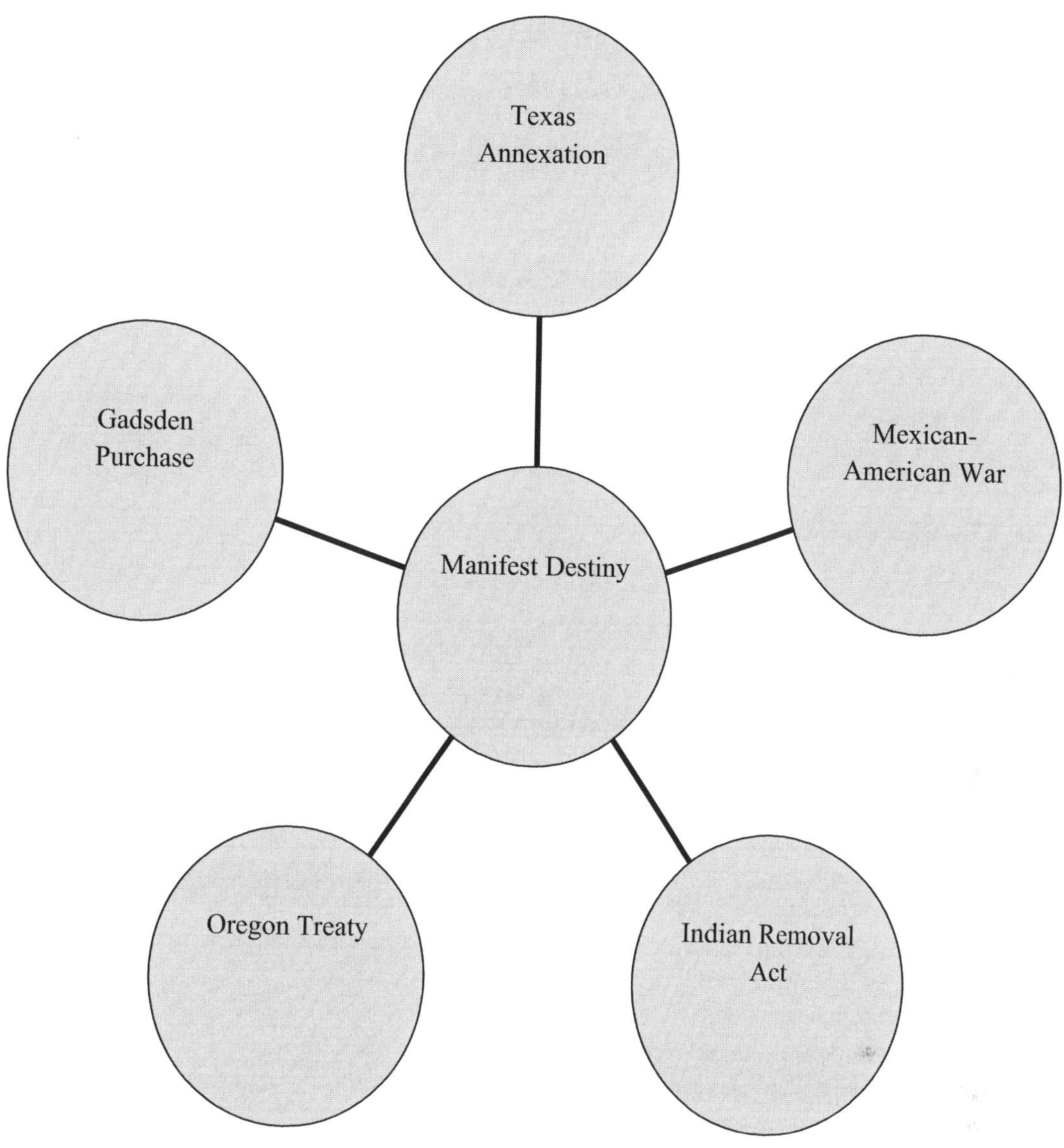
Texas
Annexation
Gadsden
Purchase
Mexican-
American War
Manifest Destiny
Oregon Treaty
Indian Removal
Act

LESSON PLAN
UNDERSTANDING DIFFERENT SOCIETIES
THE NORTH, THE MIDWEST AND THE SOUTH

Teacher:	Date:
Subject:	Period(s):
Title of Lesson:	State Standards:
Common Core Standards and Indicators: **RH.11-12.2.** Determine the central ideas or information of a primary or secondary source; provide an accurate summary that makes clear the relationships among the key details and ideas	College Readiness Standards: **ACT-CR: Reading, ACT-CR: Score Range 16–19** **Main Ideas and Author's Approach:** Identify a clear main idea or purpose of straightforward paragraphs in uncomplicated literary narratives **Supporting Details:** Locate simple details at the sentence and paragraph level in uncomplicated passages

Purpose/ Objective	To help students understand the different societies that had developed in the United States by the 1850s with an emphasis on the differences between the north and south in an effort to understand the events that led to the Civil War. This activity will target students' reading and writing skills through the identification and summarization of main ideas and supporting details.
Materials	Copies of outline notes on following pages about the North, the Midwest and the South, transparency of outline notes, textbook
Procedures	Pass out copies of the outline. Put transparency of outline on overhead projector and complete a couple of the supporting details together with the class as example. Allow students to work on outline in class for two days with teacher assistance then allow students to complete the outline for homework.
Assessment	Students can write a summary of the information contained in their completed outline or this activity can be graded as a notebook assignment.
Comments	Teacher should decide the number of supporting details students should find. Use this outline as a guide. Be sure to stress the fact most people in the South were not slave owners, and that most people who did own slaves owned five or less, thereby debunking the myth that everyone in the South owned large numbers of slaves.

The North, the Midwest and the South

I. Northern and Midwestern Societies

A. Three distinct class structures emerged in the North by the 1830s
   1. Supporting details
   2. Supporting details

B. Advancements in industrial and farming production created more jobs and wealth
   1. Supporting details
   2. Supporting details

C. Increased immigration brought more workers to America but also more resistance by native born Americans
   1. Supporting details

D. The Midwest…
   1. Supporting details

II. The South

A. The southern economy was based on agricultural, particularly cotton
   1. Supporting details – cotton gin
   2. Supporting details

B. Agricultural production and slave labor…
   1. Supporting details
   2. Supporting details

C. Though the South had some manufacturing, manufacturing never developed like it did in the North
   1. Supporting details
   2. Supporting details

D. Southern Class Structure…
   1. 72% of southern people owned less than ten slaves
   2. 34% of the southern population were slaves in 1860
   3. Supporting details

III. The Slave System

A. The South and Slavery
   1. Supporting details

B. Slave labor on the plantations was highly organized
   1. Supporting details
   2. Supporting details

C. Slave culture and religion
   1. Supporting details
   2. Supporting details

D. Slave resistance
   1. Harriet Tubman and the Underground Railroad
      a. Supporting details
   2. Supporting details

Study Guide for Rising Tensions between North and South

1. Who were Henry Clay, John C. Calhoun, Daniel Webster, Stephen Douglas, and Abraham Lincoln?
2. What issues in California and other new territories caused problems between free and slave states?
3. Explain the Compromise of 1850 and its major provisions.
4. Why was the new Fugitive Slave Act so controversial?
5. How did Daniel Webster create support for the Compromise of 1850 in his "Seventh of March" speech?
6. What was the Kansas-Nebraska Act of 1854? What problems did it solve (or create) and what political party was created in response to it?
7. Explain the idea of popular sovereignty and how it led to "Bleeding Kansas?"
8. What were the main aspects of the Republican Party platform of 1856 and 1860?
9. Explain the Dred Scott Case. What effect did it have on slavery and the country?
10. What were the major arguments of the Free Soil movement and the proslavery position?
11. Explain "King Cotton."
12. Describe the plantation system in the South. What was the Underground Railroad?
13. What was <u>Uncle Tom's Cabin</u> and what effect did it have on the North and South?
14. Why were the Lincoln-Douglas debates of 1858 important? What was the Freeport Doctrine?
15. Explain John Brown's raid on Harpers Ferry. What U.S. military man arrested him?
16. Explain how <u>Uncle Tom's Cabin</u> and John Brown's raid drove the North and South closer to war.
17. Why did some southern states threaten to secede if Lincoln was elected in 1860?
18. Explain the outcome of the election of 1860.
19. What southern states were the first to secede?
20. What were the major political, economic, and social differences between the North and South? How did each side view the other?
21. Who held most of the political power in the South before the war?
22. How many slaves were in the South and who owned most of them?
23. What happened at Fort Sumter and how did Lincoln respond?
24. Who was the president of the Confederate States of America and what states were part of the Confederacy?
25. Do you think the Civil War was avoidable?

Rising Tensions between North and South

Compromise of 1850

- To deal with the question of slavery when California applied for statehood in 1850
- Missouri Compromise line did not extend to California and there was no slave state to add to preserve balance of power in Congress
- The compromise, written by Henry Clay and supported by Daniel Webster, had to please northern anti-slavery people and southern proslavery people

<u>Terms of the Compromise of 1850</u>

- California admitted as a free state
- New Fugitive Slave Act
- Divided land from Mexican Cession into two territories with popular sovereignty
- Abolished slave trade but not slavery itself in Washington D.C.

Uncle Tom's Cabin-1852

- Book written by abolitionist Harriet Beecher Stowe about the horrors of slavery
- Fueled the abolitionist movement in the North but angered Southerners because it depicted all Southerners as evil slave masters like Simon Legree
- Greatly increased tensions between North and South

Kansas/Nebraska Act-1854

- Stephen Douglas' plan to let voters in Kansas and Nebraska decided the issue of slavery based on popular sovereignty
- Led to violence in Kansas between proslavery and antislavery settlers **(Bleeding Kansas, 1855)**
- Contradicted Missouri Compromise of 1820, which outlawed slavery in that area

Formation of the Republican Party-1854

- Antislavery Whigs, Democrats, and Free-Soilers formed this new political party to oppose the expansion of slavery

Dred Scott Case-1857

- Important Supreme Court case about slavery (Roger Taney was Chief Justice)
- Stated slaves and even free blacks were not considered citizens and therefore had no rights, including the right to sue in court
- Slaves were property and as property could be taken anywhere by their owners
- Victory for proslavery people because it indicated slavery could not be banned from the territories
- Also contradicted Missouri Compromise and even popular sovereignty

- Spilt the Democratic party even more between those who supported popular sovereignty (Stephen Douglas) and those who did not

John Brown's Raid on Harpers Ferry-1859

- Abolitionist attempted to raid a federal arsenal for weapons to start a slave uprising
- Southerners were angered and began to fear the North even more because they thought everyone in the North was a violent abolitionist like John Brown
- Greatly increased tensions between the North and South

Election of 1860

- Republicans chose Abraham Lincoln as their candidate
- Lincoln ran against Democrat Stephen Douglas and two other candidates
- Some southern states threatened to secede if Lincoln was elected
- Lincoln won the November election, and South Carolina seceded in December 1860 followed by six more states
- Seceded states formed the Confederate States of America, wrote their own constitution, and elected Jefferson Davis as their president.
- Richmond, Virginia was chosen to be the permanent capital of the Confederacy

LESSON PLAN
FREE-SOIL IDEOLOGY V. THE PRO-SLAVERY ARGUMENT

Teacher:	Date:
Subject:	Period(s):
Title of Lesson:	State Standards:
Common Core Standards and Indicators: **RH.11-12.2.** Determine the central ideas or information of a primary or secondary source; provide an accurate summary that makes clear the relationships among the key details and ideas. **RH.11-12.6.** Evaluate authors' differing points of view on the same historical event or issue by assessing the authors' claims, reasoning, and evidence.	College Readiness Standards: **ACT-CR: Reading, ACT-CR: Score Range 16–19** **Main Ideas and Author's Approach:** Identify a clear main idea or purpose of straightforward paragraphs in uncomplicated literary narratives **Generalizations and Conclusions:** Draw simple generalizations and conclusions using details that support the main points of more challenging passages

Purpose/ Objective	Students will understand the Free-Soil ideology and the pro-slavery arguments. This is necessary if students are to really understand why it became impossible for anti-slavery and pro-slavery interests to continue to compromise on the issue of slavery. Students will be asked to evaluate the strength and weakness of each point of view.
Materials	Transparency of reading activity from following page, copies of articles on the Free-Soil ideology and the pro-slavery arguments
Procedures	Pass out copies of articles to students and display transparency of activity on overhead. Go through the pre-reading questions together with class to access students' prior knowledge on slavery and get them thinking about the topic. Point out the important vocabulary terms they will encounter. Pre-teach the vocabulary terms if necessary. Have the students read the articles and answer the post-reading questions. Go over the vocabulary questions and the post-reading questions with the class.
Assessment	Post-reading questions can be collected for a grade. Students can be tested or quizzed on this information and information learned in this activity can also be used in other activities, such as the Civil War PowerPoint project.
Comments	The activity on the next page should be used as a guide since the vocabulary terms and questions a teacher might choose to emphasize might be different than the examples given. Many high school textbooks do not have sufficient information on the Free-Soil ideology or pro-slavery arguments. College and A.P. textbooks often have sections devoted to these topics that can be utilized. Otherwise, teacher should find articles from other sources that can be used for this assignment.

Free-Soil Ideology v. Pro-slavery Argument

Pre-Reading Questions

1. How long has slavery existed?
2. Why might one want to own a slave?
3. How was American chattel slavery different from other types of slavery?
4. What economic advantages does a slave owner have over one who has regular employees? Is this competition fair?

Vocabulary Terms

ideology	ambivalence	propagandists
dispersed	apologists	
static	pestilential	
entrenched	plaguing	

Post-Reading Questions

1. Why were many Northerners opposed to the expansion of slavery?
2. What ideas did the free soil or free labor position rest upon?
3. What was the abolitionist argument based upon?
4. What view did the North have of the South and vice-versa?
5. Summarize the reasons Free-Soilers did not believe in the institution of slavery?
6. Summarize the main points of the pro-slavery argument.
7. What view did many Southerners have of Northern industrial life and the life of northern workers?
8. Evaluate the strengths and weakness of each argument.
9. What political party supported the abolitionist and free-Soil ideologies?

LESSON PLAN
THE DRED SCOTT DECISION

Teacher:	Date:
Subject:	Period(s):
Title of Lesson:	State Standards:
Common Core Standards and Indicators: **RH.11-12.2.** Determine the central ideas or information of a primary or secondary source; provide an accurate summary that makes clear the relationships among the key details and ideas.	College Readiness Standards: **ACT-CR: Reading, ACT-CR: Score Range 16–19** **Main Ideas and Author's Approach:** Identify a clear main idea or purpose of straightforward paragraphs in uncomplicated literary narratives **Generalizations and Conclusions:** Draw simple generalizations and conclusions using details that support the main points of more challenging passages

Purpose/ Objective	Students will better understand the controversial Dred Scott decision by the Supreme Court and the consequences it had on the country in terms of bringing the country a major step closer to Civil War. Students will be asked to evaluate the strengths and weaknesses of the Supreme Court's decision.
Materials	Transparency of reading activity from following page, textbook, copies of articles about the Dred Scott decision
Procedures	Pass out copies of articles to students. Display transparency of activity on overhead and go through the pre-reading questions together with class to access students' prior knowledge on citizenship and slavery and to get them thinking about the topic. Point out the important vocabulary terms they will encounter. Pre-teach the vocabulary terms if necessary. Have the students read the articles and answer the post-reading questions. Go over the vocabulary questions and the post-reading questions with the class.
Assessment	Post-reading questions can be collected for a grade. Students can also be tested or quizzed on this information and information learned in this activity can also be used in other activities such as the Civil War PowerPoint project.
Comments	The activity on the next page should be used as a guide since the vocabulary terms and questions a teacher might choose to emphasize might be different than the examples given. While many high school textbooks include information on the on the Dred Scott decision, they often do not go into much detail. The teacher should find articles on the Internet or from other sources such as College or A.P. textbooks that can used for this assignment.

The Dred Scott Case

Pre-Reading Questions

1. What makes someone a citizen of this country? How is citizenship defined?
2. What is the difference between a privilege and a right?
3. What privileges or rights are associated with being a citizen?
4. What privileges or rights are denied to people who are not citizens?
5. What is private property? Are there limits as to what one can do with their property?
6. What does the 5th Amendment say about private property and due process?

Vocabulary

controversial	null and void
pilgrimage	elated
abolitionist	sanctioned
jurisdiction	preparatory
sojourn	pronouncement

Post-reading Questions

1. Why did Dred Scott think he should have his freedom?
2. What did Chief Justice Taney say about all black people and their right to take someone to court?
3. According to the Supreme Court's decision, slaves were officially classified as what?
4. How did the Court's decision affect the expansion of slavery and the Missouri Compromise?
5. What Constitutional Amendment was the basis for allowing slavery into the territories?
6. Did the Court's decision favor the pro-slavery movement or the anti-slavery movement?
7. How did the Republicans respond to the Court's decision?
8. If you were a pro-slavery southerner, what would you think of the Republican's response?
9. Was Frederick Douglas' statement a foreshadowing of things to come?
10. Why was this case so important? (How did it affect the Democratic Party? Did it increase tensions between the North and South?)

LESSON PLAN
GRAPHIC ORGANIZER
EVENTS LEADING TO THE CIVIL WAR

Teacher:	Date:
Subject:	Period(s):
Title of Lesson:	State Standards:
Common Core Standards and Indicators: **RH.11-12.2.** Determine the central ideas or information of a primary or secondary source; provide an accurate summary that makes clear the relationships among the key details and ideas	College Readiness Standards: **ACT-CR: Reading, ACT-CR: Score Range 20–23** **Sequential, Comparative, and Cause-Effect Relationships**: Identify clear relationships between people, ideas, and so on in uncomplicated passages **ACT-CR: Reading, ACT-CR: Score Range 16–19** **Generalizations and Conclusions:** Draw simple generalizations and conclusions about people, ideas, and so on in uncomplicated passages

Purpose/ Objective	Students will gain a better understanding of the events that to the American Civil War while enhancing their reading, writing, summarization, and critical thinking skills.
Materials	Copies of blank graphic organizer contained on following pages, transparency of graphic organizer completed with possible answers contained on following pages, textbook or other sources such as the Internet
Procedures	Teacher will distribute blank copies of graphic organizer to students and explain the assignment. Students are to use their textbook or other sources to complete the graphic organizer. When assignment is completed teacher should display the transparency of the completed graphic organizer on the overhead projector and go over possible answers with the students so they can check their work.
Assessment	Assignment can be graded on a standard scale with points taken off for each item missed or a rubric can be designed. Students will be quizzed and tested on this information. These notes can also serve as the basis of information for other activities such as the Civil War PowerPoint project.
Comments	Teacher can collect and grade the assignment before going over the answers or give the students a chance to correct their work by going over the answers with the students before the assignment is collected. This is always at the teacher's discretion and depends on the level of the students and difficulty of assignment. The completed graphic organizer can also be used simply as handout notes or as lecture notes.

Events Leading to the Civil War

Name______________________

Date	Event	Issue	Summary of Event	Outcome or Effect
1820	Missouri Compromise			
1850	Compromise of 1850			
1852	Uncle Tom's Cabin			
Early 1800s-1865	Underground Railroad			
1854	Kansas-Nebraska Act			
1854	Formation of the Republican Party			

Date	**Event**	**Issue**	**Summary of Event**	**Outcome or Effect**
1857	Dred Scott Case			
1858	Lincoln-Douglas Debates			
1859	John Brown's Raid on Harpers Ferry			
1860	The Election of 1860			
1860-1861	Secession of Seven Southern States			
1861	Start of Civil War at Fort Sumter			

Events Leading to the Civil War

Name____________________________

Date	Event	Issue	Summary of Event	Outcome or Effect
1820	Missouri Compromise	Missouri entering Union as slave state	Missouri enters Union as slave state, Maine as free state, and slavery outlawed north of 36°30" line through Louisiana Territory	Fight between North and South avoided for 41 years before Civil War
1850	Compromise of 1850	California entering Union as free state	California becomes free state, South gets new fugitive slave law, no more slave trade in Washington D.C., AZ and NM use popular sovereignty	Fight between North and South avoided for 11 years before Civil War
1852	Uncle Tom's Cabin	Slavery	Harriet Stowe wrote a book about the cruelties of slavery	Book angered many southerners because it depicted southerners as evil slave owners. More people in the North opposed slavery
Early 1800s-1865	Underground Railroad	Escaping from slavery	A secret system of helping slaves escape to the North using guides (conductors) and hiding places (stations)	System was hated by slave owners even though only a few thousand slaves escaped
1854	Kansas-Nebraska Act	Forming two new states out of the Louisiana Territory	Congress decided to let the people of Kansas and Nebraska territories decide on slavery for themselves (popular sovereignty)	Pro- and anti-slavery settlers clashed in Kansas (Bleeding Kansas) until Kansas became a free state in 1861. Nebraska became free state in 1867
1854	Formation of the Republican Party	Slavery expanding into the territories	Republican Party formed by those who opposed the expansion of slavery	Republican Party lost the 1856 presidential election but continued to gain support

Date	Event	Issue	Summary of Event	Outcome or Effect
1857	Dred Scott Case	Bringing a slave into free territory	Dred Scott asked Supreme Court to free him on the grounds he was once taken to free territory	Supreme Court decided black people were not citizens and slaves were property that could be taken anywhere. Northerners were outraged
1858	Lincoln-Douglas Debates	Electing a U.S. senator from Illinois (Republican Abraham Lincoln v. Democrat Stephen Douglas)	Lincoln argued against slavery and pointed out the contradiction between popular sovereignty and the Dred Scott decision (Freeport Doctrine)	Lincoln lost this election but became nationally known. Split between Democratic Party over issue of slavery widened
1859	John Brown's Raid on Harpers Ferry	Getting rid of slavery	John Brown raided an arsenal for guns and ammunition to start a slave revolt	John Brown was caught before starting the revolt and hanged. Southerners were angered and convinced northerners were out to destroy slavery
1860	The Election of 1860	Electing a new president	Lincoln (Republican) beat a northern Democrat (Stephen Douglas), a southern Democrat and a compromise candidate	Lincoln won the election even though he got no electoral votes from ten southern states
1860-1861	Secession of Seven Southern States	Splitting of the United States	After Lincoln's victory seven southern states seceded, starting with South Carolina, and formed the Confederate States of America	Lincoln was sworn in as president in March, 1861, with seven states seceded and eight more threatening to do so
1861	Start of Civil War at Fort Sumter, South Carolina	What should be done about the seceded states	President Lincoln sent supplies to Fort Sumter, and the Confederates opened fire on the fort	The fort surrendered, four more southern states seceded to join the Confederacy and both sides prepared for war

The Civil War

The Civil War

-over 618,000 people died (2% of the population) from 1861-1865
-often called "A rich man's war but a poor man's fight"
-first modern war-new weapons/tactics, ironclads, submarines, balloons, mines
-most people thought it would be a short war, but it forever changed the country

-ended slavery and idea of states' rights
-accelerated the industrialization of the country
-destroyed southern wealth and landscape

Causes

- the expansion of slavery into new territories led to the Civil War
-the free northern and proslavery southern states could no longer compromise over the issue of slavery
-seven southern states seceded when Lincoln was elected
-they formed the Confederate State of America
-first shots fired when Confederates attacked Fort Sumter, South Carolina
-four more states seceded when Lincoln called up 75,000 volunteers
-four slave states (called **border states**) remained loyal to the Union (MD, KY, MO,DE)

Union and Confederacy

-Lincoln thought the seceded states were simply states in rebellion
-Jefferson Davis elected president of the Confederacy; thought they were a separate country

War Goals

-Union fighting to restore the nation; goal of ending slavery came in 1862/63
-Confederacy was fighting for its independence (right to keep slaves)

Advantages

-North had more men, more money, more factories, more rail lines, newer technology, and Lincoln was willing to adapt to changes
-South had better generals, knew the land, and believed in their cause

Strategies

-North had to fight a harder offensive war; adopted the **Anaconda Plan**
- Blockade southern ports in the Atlantic to keep out supplies
- Control the Mississippi River

- Split the Confederacy-east from west and upper from lower
- Seize the Confederate capital of Richmond, Virginia

-South was to fight a defensive war, hope Britain or France would intervene because of cotton shortages, and hold out for a Union surrender

Generals

-Lincoln went through a series of generals until he found one he liked in Ulysses S. Grant (1864) to lead the Army of the Potomac
-other Union generals included McClellan, Hooker, Meade and Sherman
-the South and Jefferson Davis stuck with Robert E. Lee to lead the Army of Northern Virginia; other southern generals included, Thomas "Stonewall" Jackson, James Longstreet, and George Pickett

Major Battles

-First Bull Run (July 1861)-showed everyone it would be a long war

-Battle of Vicksburg (May-July 1863)-Grant took control of Mississippi River

-Antietam (September 17, 1862)

-bloodiest single day in American history
-led to the Emancipation Proclamation

-Chancellorsville (May 1863)

-Lee's greatest victory; thought he was invincible
-Lee lost his best general, Thomas "Stonewall" Jackson

-Gettysburg (July 1-3, 1862)

-bloodiest battle of war and considered the turning point

-decimated Lee's army (Pickett's Charge)

-led to the Gettysburg Address-statement of American ideals

-Atlanta (September 1864)

-Sherman captured and burned Atlanta

-helped Lincoln win re-election in November, 1864

-started Sherman's March to the Sea and "scorched earth" policy

-divided upper and lower South

-Wilderness, Cold Harbor & Spotsylvania were bloody battles in 1864-1865

Emancipation Proclamation

Lincoln considered adding the possibility of freeing the slaves as a second war goal in 1862

Reasons for emancipation

-morally right thing to do
-use war to bring about this change
-military benefits if ex-slaves joined the Union army (180,000+ did)
-hurt the southern labor force (as slaves deserted southern fields there was no one to work the land)

Problems

-Lincoln had to be careful Border States would not secede
-Could not make it look like a move out of desperation- needed Union victory

Solutions

-Wait for a victory on the battlefield (Antietam-September, 17 1862)
-Officially signed January 1st 1863
-Emancipation Proclamation only pertained to areas still in rebellion

Effects

-angered many northerners who did not want to fight to end slavery (draft riots broke out)
-pleased many abolitionists who had been calling for an end to slavery for a long time
-added second goal to war that people would come to embrace over time (slavery made South strong)
-huge military advantage for North, created major labor and economic problems for South
-removed possibility of France or England helping Confederacy (those countries opposed slavery)
-Border States and other southern areas controlled by Union remained loyal to Union

The official and complete end of slavery would not come until the 13th Amendment was adopted after the war.

Election of 1864

Lincoln and his Republican Party faced major criticism in 1864 because the war had dragged on so long and because of the enormous loss of life.

Though many northern Democrats had originally supported the northern cause of preserving the Union, by 1864 a faction of northern Democrats called for an immediate end to the war and a peace settlement with the Confederacy. In 1864, they chose George B. McClellan, the former head of the Union Army, to run against Lincoln.

These northern Democrats were known as "Peace Democrats." Many Republicans called them "**Copperheads**" and labeled them as being disloyal.

Lincoln was aware of the growing anti-war sentiment in the North but remained determined to settle for nothing less than an all-out Union victory. There would be no compromise.

In 1864, it was decided to switch the Republican Party name (not the party's beliefs) and run under a new name. For the election of 1864 Lincoln ran under the Union Party (1864-1868). Andrew Johnson from Tennessee was chosen to run as his Vice-President, replacing Hannibal Hamlin who was from Maine. The Union Party was supported by northern War Democrats, and Andrew Johnson was the only other Union president.

While the public questioned Lincoln's strategies, the soldiers were extremely loyal to Lincoln because he wanted to fight to win and did not want the war to have been in vain. Over 70% of soldiers voted for Lincoln.

General Sherman's capture of Atlanta in September 1864 was a major Union victory that directly helped Lincoln win re-election in November. During the election Sherman gave leave to thousands of his soldiers so they could go back home and vote for Lincoln.

Results of the Civil War

The North (Union) won the war, the Confederacy was destroyed, and our country was preserved

Over 600,000 American lives were lost and slavery was ended

The federal government became more powerful, and the idea of states' rights died

The question of whether or not a state could secede from the Union was answered by the North winning (NO!)

Much of the southern landscape and economy was destroyed

The Civil War sped up industrialization, especially in the North-(large scale machine-driven manufacturing made possible by new inventions)

13th , 14th, and 15th Amendments passed

13th-Abolished slavery

14th-Defined citizenship and made all black people official citizens of the U.S.

15th-Gave black males the right to vote

Ex-slaves and free blacks enjoyed more freedom but still faced discrimination and obstacles associated with lack of skills and education. Many simply continued as poor farmers in the South and faced racist segregation laws (Jim Crow laws)

LESSON PLAN
GETTYSBURG ADDRESS ACTIVITY

Teacher:	Date:
Subject:	Period(s):
Title of Lesson:	State Standards:
Common Core Standards and Indicators: **RH.11-12.2.** Determine the central ideas or information of a primary or secondary source; provide an accurate summary that makes clear the relationships among the key details and ideas; **RH.11-12.4.** Determine the meaning of words and phrases as they are used in a text, including analyzing how an author uses and refines the meaning of a key term over the course of a text (e.g., how Madison defines faction in Federalist No. 10).	College Readiness Standards: **ACT-CR: Reading, ACT-CR: Score Range 24–27** **Meanings of Words:** Use context to determine the appropriate meaning of some figurative and nonfigurative words, phrases, and statements in more challenging passages **ACT-CR: Reading, ACT-CR: Score Range 20–23** **Generalizations and Conclusions:** Draw simple generalizations and conclusions using details that support the main points of more challenging passages

Purpose/ Objective	Students will learn why the Gettysburg Address became one of the most important speeches in American history and how Lincoln's words expressed the importance of this battle not only to the Civil War but also the importance of the Civil War to the country. Students will also understand both the literal and figurative references in the speech, which characterized the ideals the nation was founded upon.
Materials	Transparency and copies of the Gettysburg Address such as the one on the following page
Procedures	Pass out copies of Gettysburg Address to students and place a transparency of the Gettysburg Address on the overhead projector. Ask students what they remember about the battle from their studies. Allow students to read through it once by themselves. Teacher will read speech aloud while stopping and asking students what they think each line or phrase means both literally and figuratively (students should be taking notes). Make connections to other documents in the nation's past, such as the Declaration of Independence and the Constitution. After going through entire speech call on students to try to summarize parts of the speech based on what they just learned. Remind students they might be asked questions about the speech on a test.
Assessment	For homework have students summarize speech in their own words based on what they learned in class.
Comments	Be sure to explain such terms as *proposition, conceived, consecrate, hallow, devotion*, "*last full measure of devotion*," *resolve*, and *in vain*.

The Gettysburg Address

Gettysburg, Pennsylvania

November 19, 1863

Four score and seven years ago our fathers brought forth on this continent, a new nation, conceived in liberty, and dedicated to the proposition that all men are created equal.

Now we are engaged in a great civil war, testing whether that nation, or any nation so conceived and so dedicated, can long endure. We are met on a great battlefield of that war. We have come to dedicated a portion of that field as a final resting place for those who here gave their lives that that nation might live. It is altogether fitting and proper that we should do this.

But, in a larger sense, we cannot dedicate—we cannot consecrate—we cannot hallow—this ground. The brave men, leaving and dead, who struggled here, have consecrated it, far above our poor power to add or detract. The world will little note, nor long remember what we say here, but it is for the living, rather, to be dedicated here to the unfinished work, which they who fought here have thus far so nobly advanced. It is rather for us to be here dedicated to the great task remaining before us—that from these honored dead we take increased devotion to that cause for which they gave the last full measure of devotion—that we here highly resolve that these dead shall not have died in vein—that this nation, under God, shall have a new birth of freedom—and that government of the people, by the people, for the people, shall not perish from the earth.

LESSON PLAN
LINCOLN'S SECOND INAUGURAL ADDRESS

Teacher:	Date:
Subject:	Period(s):
Title of Lesson:	State Standards:
Common Core Standards and Indicators: **RH.11-12.2.** Determine the central ideas or information of a primary or secondary source; provide an accurate summary that makes clear the relationships among the key details and ideas; **RH.11-12.4.** Determine the meaning of words and phrases as they are used in a text, including analyzing how an author uses and refines the meaning of a key term over the course of a text (e.g., how Madison defines faction in Federalist No. 10).	College Readiness Standards: **ACT-CR: Reading, ACT-CR: Score Range 24–27** **Meanings of Words:** Use context to determine the appropriate meaning of some figurative and nonfigurative words, phrases, and statements in more challenging passages **ACT-CR: Reading, ACT-CR: Score Range 20–23** **Generalizations and Conclusions:** Draw simple generalizations and conclusions using details that support the main points of more challenging passages

Purpose/ Objective	Students will learn why Lincoln's Second Inaugural Address became one of the most important speeches in American history and how Lincoln's words, literal and figurative, characterized a nation torn apart by war with the uneasy task of rebuilding itself still ahead.
Materials	Transparency and copies of Lincoln's Second Inaugural Address such as the one on the following page
Procedures	Pass out copies of Lincoln's Second Inaugural Address to students and place a transparency of it on the overhead projector. Allow students to read through it once by themselves. Teacher will read the speech aloud while stopping and asking students what they think each line or phrase means both literally and figuratively (students should be taking notes). Ask students what they think Lincoln is trying to accomplish in his speech… Is he trying to blame and alienate the people of the South or reconcile with them? Is his tone one of harshness or regret and reconciliation? Why? After going through entire speech call on students to try to summarize parts of the speech based on what they just learned.
Assessment	Remind students they might be asked questions about the speech on a test. Students could also be asked to outline or summarize the speech for homework.
Comments	Be sure to explain such terms as *engrosses, prediction, ventured, dissolved, deprecated, perish, constituted, discern, fervently, and malice.*

The Second Inaugural Address of Abraham Lincoln (March 4, 1865)

Fellow Countrymen:

At this second appearing to take the oath of the presidential office, there is less occasion for an extended address than there was at the first. Then a statement, somewhat in detail, of a course to be pursued, seemed fitting and proper. Now, at the expiration of four years, during which public declarations have been constantly called forth on every point and phase of the great contest which still absorbs the attention and engrosses the energies of the nation, little that is new could be presented. The progress of our arms, upon which all else chiefly depends, is as well known to the public as to myself; and it is, I trust, reasonably satisfactory and encouraging to all. With high hope for the future, no prediction in regard to it is ventured.

On the occasion corresponding to this four years ago, all thoughts were anxiously directed to an impending civil war. All dreaded it; all sought to avert it. While the inaugural address was being delivered from this place, devoted altogether to saving the Union without war, insurgent agents were in the city seeking to destroy it without war--seeking to dissolve the Union and divide effects by negotiation. Both parties deprecated war, but one of them would make war rather than let the nation survive; and the other would accept war rather than let it perish. And the war came.

One-eighth of the whole population were colored slaves, not distributed generally over the Union, but localized in the southern part of it. These slaves constituted a peculiar and powerful interest. All knew that this interest was, somehow, the cause of the war. To strengthen, perpetuate, and extend this interest was the object for which the insurgents would rend the Union even by war, while the government claimed no right to do more than to restrict the territorial enlargement of it. Neither party expected for the war the magnitude or the duration which it has already attained. Neither anticipated that the cause of the conflict might cease with, or even before, the conflict itself should cease. Each looked for an easier triumph, and a result less fundamental and astounding. Both read the same Bible and pray to the same God, and each invokes His aid against the other. It may seem strange that any men should dare to ask a just God's assistance in wringing their bread from the sweat of other men's faces, but let us judge not, that we be not judged. The prayers of both could not be answered. That of neither has been answered fully. The Almighty has His own purposes. "Woe unto the world because of offenses; for it must needs be that offenses come, but woe to that man by whom the offense cometh." If we shall suppose that American slavery is one of those offenses which, in the providence of God, must needs come, but which, having continued through His appointed time, He now wills to remove, and that He gives to both North and South this terrible war as the woe due to those by whom the offense came, shall we discern therein any departure from those divine attributes which the believers in a living God always ascribe to Him? Fondly do we hope, fervently do we pray, that this mighty scourge of war may speedily pass away. Yet, if God wills that it continue until all the wealth piled by the bondsman's two hundred and fifty years of unrequited toil shall be sunk, and until every drop of blood drawn with the lash shall be paid by another drawn with the sword, as was said three thousand years ago, so still it must be said "the judgments of the Lord are true and righteous altogether."

With malice toward none, with charity for all, with firmness in the right as God gives us to see the right, let us strive on to finish the work we are in, to bind up the nation's wounds, to care for him who shall have borne the battle and for his widow and his orphan, to do all which may achieve and cherish a just and lasting peace among ourselves and with all nations.

LESSON PLAN
CIVIL WAR MAP ASSIGNMENT

<table>
<tr><td colspan="2">Teacher:</td><td>Date:</td></tr>
<tr><td colspan="2">Subject:</td><td>Period(s):</td></tr>
<tr><td colspan="2">Title of Lesson:</td><td>State Standards:</td></tr>
<tr><td colspan="2">Common Core Standards and Indicators:
RH.11-12.7. Integrate and evaluate multiple sources of information presented in diverse formats and media (e.g., visually, quantitatively, as well as in words) in order to address a question or solve a problem.</td><td>College Readiness Standards:
ACT-CR: Reading, ACT-CR: Score Range 16–19
Generalizations and Conclusions: Draw simple generalizations and conclusions about people, ideas, and so on in uncomplicated passages</td></tr>
<tr><td>Purpose/ Objective</td><td colspan="2">Students will strengthen their geography and map reading skills while learning more about the Civil War and some of its important battles.</td></tr>
<tr><td>Materials</td><td colspan="2">Assignment directions from next page, colored pencils, textbook, blank outline map of the United States</td></tr>
<tr><td>Procedures</td><td colspan="2">Pass out copies of the map directions contained on the following page.

Allow students to work on map activity in class for a day or two and complete the rest for homework.

If desired, play Civil War-era music in the background while students work on their maps.</td></tr>
<tr><td>Assessment</td><td colspan="2">This assignment can be graded by creating a rubric or simply grading it on a sliding scale. Teacher will determine the point value of the assignment. Points are subtracted for every item missing.</td></tr>
<tr><td>Comments</td><td colspan="2">Two sets of directions are contained on one page to save paper. Copy directions and cut into slips. More points should be subtracted for the more important or more time- consuming items required for the assignment.</td></tr>
</table>

Civil War Map Assignment

You are to make a map of the United States during the Civil War. Include the following items on your map. Use the maps in the chapter as a guide.

1. Use three different colors to label the Union states, the border states, and the Confederate States of America.
2. Label where the war started at Fort Sumter and include a date.
3. Label Washington D.C. and the Confederate capital of Richmond
4. Outline the parts of the Anaconda Plan (use numbers on your map and key to designate parts)
5. Label the battles of Bull Run, Antietam, Fredericksburg, Chancellorsville, Vicksburg, Gettysburg, Cold Harbor, and the naval battle between the ironclads Monitor and Merrimack
6. Put dates next to all battles and designate who won with a "U" or "C"
7. Trace Sherman's March to the Sea beginning from Chattanooga to Atlanta to Savannah
8. Highlight Sherman's "scorched earth" strategy by putting flames along his path after Atlanta
9. Label the town where the war ended along with the date
10. Make a map key and attach this sheet to the map with completed items checked off.

Civil War Map Assignment

You are to make a map of the United States during the Civil War. Include the following items on your map. Use the maps in the chapter as a guide.

1. Use three different colors to label the Union states, the border states, and the Confederate States of America.
2. Label where the war started at Fort Sumter and include a date.
3. Label Washington D.C. and the Confederate capital of Richmond
4. Outline the parts of the Anaconda Plan (use numbers on your map and key to designate parts)
5. Label the battles of Bull Run, Antietam, Fredericksburg, Chancellorsville, Vicksburg, Gettysburg, Cold Harbor, and the naval battle between the ironclads Monitor and Merrimack
6. Put dates next to all battles and designate who won with a "U" or "C"
7. Trace Sherman's March to the Sea beginning from Chattanooga to Atlanta to Savannah
8. Highlight Sherman's "scorched earth" strategy by putting flames along his path after Atlanta
9. Label the town where the war ended along with the date
10. Make a map key and attach this sheet to the map with completed items checked off.

LESSON PLAN
CIVIL WAR BATTLE TABLE

Teacher:	Date:
Subject:	Period(s):
Title of Lesson:	State Standards:
Common Core Standards and Indicators: **RH.11-12.7.** Integrate and evaluate multiple sources of information presented in diverse formats and media (e.g., visually, quantitatively, as well as in words) in order to address a question or solve a problem.	College Readiness Standards: **ACT-CR: Reading, ACT-CR: Score Range 13–15** **Supporting Details:** Locate basic facts (e.g., names, dates, events) clearly stated in a passage

Purpose/ Objective	Students will gain a better understanding of some of the major battles of the American Civil War.
Materials	Copies of blank graphic organizer contained on following pages, transparency of graphic organizer completed with answers contained on following pages, textbook, and other sources of battle data such that can be found on the Internet
Procedures	Teacher will distribute blank copies of the graphic organizer to students and explain the assignment. Students are to use their textbook and other sources to complete the graphic organizer. When assignment is completed teacher should display the transparency of the completed graphic organizer on the overhead projector and go over possible answers with the students so they can check their work.
Assessment	Assignment can be graded on a standard scale with points taken off for each item missed or a rubric can be designed. These notes will also serve as the basis of information for other activities such as the Civil War Excel Project II. This assignment will be needed for the Civil War Excel Assignment II.
Comments	Websites such as civilwarhome.com/battles.htm, civilwarhome.com/record.htm and americancivilwar.com are quite useful for this activity. Names in parentheses are the alternate names for some of the battles. Numbers often vary slightly by source of the data. This assignment will be needed for the Civil War Excel Assignment II.

Civil War Battle Table

	Location	**Date**	**General**	**Victor**	**Casualties**	**Importance**
1st Bull Run (1st Manassas)						
Shiloh (Pittsburg Landing)						
New Orleans						
2nd Bull Run (2nd Manassas)						
Antietam (Sharpsburg)						
Fredericksburg						

	Location	Date	General	Victor	Casualties	Importance
Chancellorsville						
Vicksburg						
Gettysburg						
Chickamauga						
Chattanooga						
Wilderness						

Civil War Battle Table

	Location	Date	General	Victor	Casualties	Importance
1st Bull Run (1st Manassas)	Manassas, Virginia	July 4, 1861	Irvin McDowell P.G.T. Beauregard	South	North 2900 South 2000	Union spurred to more effort, South gained confidence
Shiloh (Pittsburg Landing)	Tennessee	April 6-7, 1862	Ulysses S. Grant Albert S. Johnson/ P.G.T. Beauregard	North	13,573 10,699	A major victory on the Mississippi
New Orleans	Louisiana	April 25, 1862	D.G. Farragut No major confederate forces just forts	North	None for Union 37 total	Major naval victory for Union on Mississippi River., captured major port city.
2nd Bull Run (2nd Manassas)	Manassas, Virginia	August 29-30, 1862	George B. McCellan Robert E. Lee	South	14,500 9,500 23,186	Made possible Lee's invasion of North at Antietam
Antietam (Sharpsburg)	Maryland	September 17, 1862	George B. McClellan Robert E. Lee	Tactical victory for the North	12,469 25,899	Repelled Lee's 1st invasion of the North, led to Emancipation Proclamation
Fredericksburg	Virginia	December 13-15, 1862	Ambrose E. Burnside Robert E. Lee	South	1284 Killed 9600 Wounded 595 Killed 4061 Wounded	Union suffered terrible casualties and Union move on Richmond was stopped

	Location	Date	General	Victor	Casualties	Importance
Chancellorsville	Virginia	May 2-4, 1863	Joseph Hooker Robert E. Lee	South	North 16,030 South 12,281	Jackson killed, made possible Lee's invasion of North at Gettysburg
Vicksburg	Mississippi	Siege May 18- July 4, 1863	Grant/ Farragut John Pemberton	North	4,536 31,277	Gained control of Mississippi River, South surrenders
Gettysburg	Pennsylvania	July 1-3, 1863	George Meade/ Joshua Chamberlain R.E. Lee J. Longstreet G. Pickett	North	23,186 31,621	Turning point of war, destroyed South's offensive strategy. Chamberlain because hero after Little Round Top
Chickamauga	Tennessee	September 19-20, 1863	William Rosecrans Braxton Bragg	South	15,581 17,804	North had to retreat to Chattanooga where South was defeated
Chattanooga	Tennessee	November 23-25, 1863	Grant Bragg	North	5,616 8684	South had to evacuate to Tennessee. Later made Sherman's march to Atlanta possible
Wilderness	Virginia	May 5-6, 1864	Grant Lee	North	37,737 11,400	Showed Grant would not retreat

LESSON PLAN
CIVIL WAR EXCEL PROJECT I

<table>
<tr><td colspan="2">Teacher:</td><td>Date:</td></tr>
<tr><td colspan="2">Subject:</td><td>Period(s):</td></tr>
<tr><td colspan="2">Title of Lesson:</td><td>State Standards:</td></tr>
<tr><td colspan="2">Common Core Standards and Indicators:
RH.9-10.7. Integrate quantitative or technical analysis (e.g., charts, research data) with qualitative analysis in print or digital text
RH.11-12.7. Integrate and evaluate multiple sources of information presented in diverse formats and media (e.g., visually, quantitatively, as well as in words) in order to address a question or solve a problem</td><td>College Readiness Standards:
ACT-CR: Reading, ACT-CR: Score Range 16–19
Generalizations and Conclusions: Draw simple generalizations and conclusions about people, ideas, and so on in uncomplicated passages</td></tr>
<tr><td>Purpose/ Objective</td><td colspan="2">To enhance students' knowledge of the American Civil War while also teaching them how to use Microsoft Excel.</td></tr>
<tr><td>Materials</td><td colspan="2">Project directions contained on the following page, textbook, Internet, other teacher-supplied resources, LCD projector, computer with Microsoft Excel</td></tr>
<tr><td>Procedures</td><td colspan="2">Divide the students into cooperative groups.

Pass out copies of directions for the project. Explain the directions.

Display a sample Excel spreadsheet to the class using a computer and LCD projector. Explain how to set up the spreadsheet using the examples given on the second page of the directions. Explain the basic mathematical functions of Excel to students and show them some simple formulas. Students should take notes on how to set up their spreadsheet.</td></tr>
<tr><td>Assessment</td><td colspan="2">Teacher will determine how many points this project is worth and can grade it using a rubric or a sliding scale.</td></tr>
<tr><td>Comments</td><td colspan="2">A working knowledge of Excel is required by the teacher. Examples of how to set up the spreadsheet are included with the directions, but the mathematical formulas are not. Figuring out how to write the formulas in the proper cells will be part of the students' learning curve though the teacher should help them with this by giving them some examples.</td></tr>
</table>

Civil War Excel Project I

Microsoft Excel is an extremely powerful and versatile database program used by people all over the world. It has countless types of personal, business, and educational applications. Excel's pages, or spreadsheets, are used to collect, organize, manipulate, and display a variety of information. It is used to keep track of personal information such as names and addresses, which can be used to create letters and mailings. It is used to track business inventory, sort and calculate mathematical data, and keep lists of information that can be imported into other programs. Excel can also use the information in its database to create charts, graphs, and other graphic representations of information to facilitate the further analysis of the data.

In our class you are going to use Microsoft Excel to collect information on the American antebellum era. You will research information related to cotton production and slavery in the South. Once your teacher shows you how to set up the Excel spreadsheet you are to enter the required information you will research then graph the results.

Resources/Websites: textbook, Internet, other teacher provided resources

Steps:

1. Research the amount of cotton production (in bales or as percentage of exports) for each decade between 1800 and 1860.

2. Research the growth in slave population for each decade between 1790 and 1860 both in terms of actual numbers and percentage of total population.

3. Research slave ownership by household in 1860 both in terms of actual numbers and percentage of southern population (no slaves, 1-4 slaves, 5-10 slaves, less then 50 slaves, 50-99 slaves, 100 or more slaves).

4. Set up your Microsoft Excel categories (columns and rows) using the information you have collected. Use separate Excel Sheets for steps 1-3.

5. Write a simple mathematical formula to make the program calculate the totals in each category. Use the program to display the results on a chart or graph.

6. Use the graphs and analysis questions to draw conclusions about cotton production and slavery and be able to explain those conclusions to the class.

Civil War Excel Project I

Sample Excel Spreadsheets

#1

	A	B	C	D	E	F	G	H	I
1		1800	1810	1820	1830	1840	1850	1860	
2	Cotton								
3									
4									
5									

#2

	A	B	C	D	E	F	G	H	I
1		1790	1800	1810	1820	1830	1840	1850	1860
2	Slave Population								
3	Percentage of Population								
4									

#3

	A	B	C	D	E	F	G	H	I
1		No Slaves	1-4 Slaves	5-10 Slaves	49- 50 Slaves	50-99 Slaves	100 or More	200 or More	
2	Slaves Per Household in 1860								
3	Percentage of Southern Population								
4									

Analysis Questions

1. What does the chart tell you about the stereotype that everyone in the South owned slaves?
2. What is the largest group in terms of percentage of population?
3. What is total number of people who owned no slaves at all?
4. Why do you think only a small number of people owned large numbers of slaves?
5. How does your chart support the notion the Civil War was a "Rich man's war but a poor man's fight?"

LESSON PLAN
CIVIL WAR EXCEL PROJECT II

<table>
<tr><td colspan="2">Teacher:</td><td>Date:</td></tr>
<tr><td colspan="2">Subject:</td><td>Period(s):</td></tr>
<tr><td colspan="2">Title of Lesson:</td><td>State Standards:</td></tr>
<tr><td colspan="2">Common Core Standards and Indicators:
RH.9-10.7. Integrate quantitative or technical analysis (e.g., charts, research data) with qualitative analysis in print or digital text
RH.11-12.7. Integrate and evaluate multiple sources of information presented in diverse formats and media (e.g., visually, quantitatively, as well as in words) in order to address a question or solve a problem</td><td>College Readiness Standards:
ACT-CR: Reading, ACT-CR: Score Range 16–19
Generalizations and Conclusions: Draw simple generalizations and conclusions about people, ideas, and so on in uncomplicated passages</td></tr>
<tr><td>Purpose/ Objective</td><td colspan="2">To enhance students' knowledge of the American Civil War while also teaching them how to use Microsoft Excel.</td></tr>
<tr><td>Materials</td><td colspan="2">Project directions contained on the following page, textbook, Internet, other teacher-supplied resources, LCD projector, computer with Microsoft Excel, Civil War Battle Table from previous activity (pages 149-153)</td></tr>
<tr><td>Procedures</td><td colspan="2">Divide the students into cooperative groups.

Pass out copies of directions for the project. Explain the directions.

Display a sample Excel spreadsheet to the class using a computer and LCD projector. Explain how to set up the spreadsheet using the examples given on the second page of the directions. Explain the basic mathematical functions of Excel to students and show them some simple formulas. Students should take notes on how to set up their spreadsheet.</td></tr>
<tr><td>Assessment</td><td colspan="2">Teacher will determine how many points this project is worth and can grade it using a rubric or a sliding scale.</td></tr>
<tr><td>Comments</td><td colspan="2">A working knowledge of Excel is required by the teacher. Examples of how to set up the spreadsheet are included with the directions, but the mathematical formulas are not. Figuring out how to write the formulas in the proper cells will be part of the students' learning curve though the teacher should help them with this by giving them some examples.</td></tr>
</table>

Civil War Excel Project II

Microsoft Excel is an extremely powerful and versatile database program used by people all over the world. It has countless types of personal, business, and educational applications. Excel's pages, or spreadsheets, are used to collect, organize, manipulate, and display a variety of information. It is used to keep track of personal information such as names and addresses, which can be used to create letters and mailings. It is used to track business inventory, sort and calculate mathematical data, and keep lists of information that can be imported into other programs. Excel can also use the information in its database to create charts, graphs, and other graphic representations of information to facilitate the further analysis of the data.

In our class you are going to use Microsoft Excel to collect information on various Civil War battles then use the program to create charts and graphs that display battlefield information, such as the number of casualties each side suffered. Once your teacher shows you how to set up the Excel spreadsheet you are to enter the required battlefield information you will research then graph the results.

Resources/Websites: civilwarhome.com/battles.htm, civilwarhome.com/record.htm, americancivilwar.com

Battles to Include: 1st Bull Run, Antietam, Fredericksburg, Chancellorsville, Gettysburg, Cold Harbor, Wilderness

Steps:

1. Research the total number of soldiers engaged and the total number of casualties for each battle for both the Union and Confederacy. Record the information on your Civil War Battle Table.

2. Set up your Microsoft Excel categories (columns and rows) with the total number engaged and the total casualties for the Union and Confederacy using the information you have already collected. Include the date and location of each battle.

3. Write a simple mathematical formula to make the program calculate the total loses in each category.

4. Use the program to display the results on a chart or graph.

5. Use your graphs and the analysis questions to draw conclusions about the battles and explain those conclusions to the class.

Civil War Excel Project II

Sample Excel Spreadsheet

	A	B	C	D	E	F
1		Union Engaged	Total Union Casualties	Confederates Engaged	Confederate Casualties	
2	1st Bull Run (7/21/1861)					
3	Antietam (9/17/1862)					
4	Fredericksburg (12/13-12/15, 1862)					
5	Gettysburg (7/1-7/3, 1863)					
6	Totals					

Analysis Questions

1. What does the total number of soldiers engaged in the battles tell you about any advantages one side had over the other? Who had more soldiers?

2. Did the number of soldiers engaged in the battles stay the same as the war continued into 1864 and 1865? If not, why were the numbers different and what does that tell you about how this became a war of attrition?

3. Which side had the advantage the longer the war continued? Why?

LESSON PLAN
CIVIL WAR POWERPOINT PROJECT

Teacher:		Date:
Subject:		Period(s):
Title of Lesson:		State Standards:
Common Core Standards and Indicators: **RH.11-12.2.** Determine the central ideas or information of a primary or secondary source; provide an accurate summary that makes clear the relationships among the key details and ideas		College Readiness Standards: **ACT-CR: Reading, ACT-CR: Score Range 16–19 Generalizations and Conclusions:** Draw simple generalizations and conclusions about people, ideas, and so on in uncomplicated passages
Purpose/ Objective	To enhance students' knowledge of the American Civil War through the use of Microsoft PowerPoint while also enhancing their presentation skills.	
Materials	Project directions contained on following page; textbook; Internet; notes, graphic organizers, and any other materials used in the student's study of the Civil War; computer and LCD projector	
Procedures	Divide class into cooperative groups. Pass out and explain project directions and grading scale. Show students the basics of using PowerPoint such as how to choose slide layouts and backgrounds, slide transitions, special effects, etc. Using computer and LCD projector show students examples of good PowerPoint slides for this project.	
Assessment	Project can be graded using the sample rubric provided or teacher can create a more detailed rubric.	
Comments	A basic working knowledge of PowerPoint is required by teacher. Do not assume all students know how to use PowerPoint. Give students a couple weeks to work on this project then have them present their projects to the class. Projects can be emailed to the teacher by assigned due date for grading. Consider an optional presentation grade.	

Group Members____

Group Civil War Slide Show Project

The Civil War was a very important event in the history of the United States. The war divided the country between North and South and put an end to slavery in this country. The purpose of this project is to help you understand the major events that led up to the Civil War, the causes of the war, and the results of the war. Students are encouraged to use other sources of information besides the textbook for this project, including the Internet, encyclopedia, and other history books.

You are to work in groups of four and make a slide show presentation of the Civil War era. The work must be evenly divided among all members (5-6 events per person). All events/topics listed below must be included and must be in chronological order. You are to make a slide for each event/topic. Each slide should be done on Microsoft PowerPoint. Each slide should be numbered and include a heading at the top of the page, some type of picture, drawing, graph or photograph in the middle of the page representing the event/topic; and a paragraph explaining the event/topic at the bottom of the page. The paragraph should include a summary of the event, why it was important, and important names and dates. Your project should include a cover page with the names of the people in your group. The last slide should include a timeline of all the events in your slide show. This instruction sheet should be handed in with your project.

Events/Topics

Compromise of 1850
The Fugitive Slave Law
The Abolitionist Movement
Uncle Tom's Cabin
Kansas-Nebraska Act and Bleeding Kansas
Republican Party Platform (what they stood for)
The Dred Scott Decision
John Brown's Raid on Harper's Ferry
Election of 1860
Creation of the Confederate States of America
Causes of the War
Attack on Fort Sumter
Advantages of each side
Presidents and Important Generals
Battle of Antietam
The Emancipation Proclamation
Battle of Gettysburg
Gettysburg Address
Sherman's March to the Sea
The Role of Women in the War
End of the War at Appomattox
Assassination of Lincoln
Results of the War
The 13th, 14th, 15th Amendments

Grading Scale

Categories	Points Possible	Points Earned
Completion of all slides	25	
Accuracy of information	25	
Creativity	25	
Overall Presentation	25	
Total	100	

Civil War Era Test

1. The Compromise of 1850
   a. admitted California as a free state
   b admitted California as a slave state
   c. required a new fugitive slave law
   d. a and c
   e. b and c

2. Who wrote the Compromise of 1850
   a. Henry Clay b. Abraham Lincoln c. John Brown d. Daniel Webster

3. According to the Fugitive Slave Law
   a. runaway slaves had to be retuned to their owners
   b. slaves in the Mexican Territories were free
   c. slaves were to be considered property
   d. slaves were free once they were North of the Missouri Compromise line

4. The system for guiding slaves to safety was
   a. Long Drive b. Final Solution c. Abolition Trail d. Underground Railroad

5. Who wrote Uncle Tom's Cabin
   a. Frederick Douglas b. Harriet Tubman c. Sojourner Truth d. Harriet Beecher Stowe

6. Popular Sovereignty was
   a. the idea that people liked to be free
   b. leaving it up to the people of a territory to decide on slavery
   c. leaving it up to the people of a territory to decide on taxes
   d. the idea of giving land back to Mexico

7. The Kansas-Nebraska Act
   a. created two new territories
   b. used the idea of popular sovereignty to decide the issue of slavery
   c. made slavery possible where it was once outlawed
   d. all of the above
   e. none of the above

8. The Kansas-Nebraska Act

   a. led to the formation of the Republican Party
   b. was created by Stephen Douglas
   c. overturned the Missouri Compromise
   d. all of the above
   e. none of the above

9. Bleeding Kansas referred to

   a. slavery being allowed in Kansas
   b. violence in Kansas between pro-slavery people and free-Soilers
   c. neither a nor b

10. According to the Dred Scott case

    a. slaves were property
    b. slaves could not sue in federal court
    c. slavery was allowed in the territories
    d. all of the above
    e. none of the above

11. Dred Scott won his case

    a. True b. False

12. In the South most political power was held by

    a. small farmers
    b. foreigners
    c. plantation owners
    d. merchants

13. Most people in the South owned slaves

    a. True b. False

14. Slaves managed to keep parts of the African Culture by

    a. singing songs b. writing letters c. reading books d. visiting Africa

15. Abraham Lincoln promised Americans he would end slavery everywhere if elected President

    a. True b. False

16. South Carolina threatened to secede if Lincoln was elected

    a. True b. False

17. The President of the Confederate States was

a. Abe Lincoln b. Robert E. Lee c. Roger Taney d. Jefferson Davis

18. States that permitted slavery but remained loyal to the Union were called

a. Confederate States b. Border States c. Union States d. Gypsy Moth States

19. The main general of the Confederacy was

a. William Sherman b. Robert E. Lee c. Stonewall Jackson d. Jefferson Davis

20. The Emancipation Proclamation

a. ended slavery everywhere
b. freed the slaves in the Border States
c. freed the slaves in the new territories
d. freed the slaves in areas in rebellion against the United States

21. The battle of Antietam allowed Lincoln to issue the Emancipation Proclamation

a. True b. False

22. The turning point in the war was

a. the battle of Antietam
b. the battle of Gettysburg
c. the Emancipation Proclamation
d. the battle of Bull Run

23. A Union greenback was a kind of

a. weapon b. soldier c. tax d. money

24. Lee surrendered to Grant at which city?

a. Atlanta b. Richmond c. Gettysburg d. Appomattox Courthouse

25. The Civil War lasted from

a. 1861 to 1865 b. 1860-1865 c. 1861-1864 d. 1850-1865

26. The North's main war strategy was called

a. Anaconda Plan b. Gettysburg Address c. Rebel Yell d. Operation Overlord

27. The permanent capital of the Confederacy was at

    a. Atlanta   b. Richmond   c. Washington D.C.   d. Gettysburg

28. The first shots of the Civil War were fired at

    a. Gettysburg   b. Antietam   c. Fort Sumter   d. Richmond

29. Who won the Civil War?

    a. North   b. South

30. The main goal of the North was to preserve the Union

    a. True   b. False

Label the Timeline (#31-40)

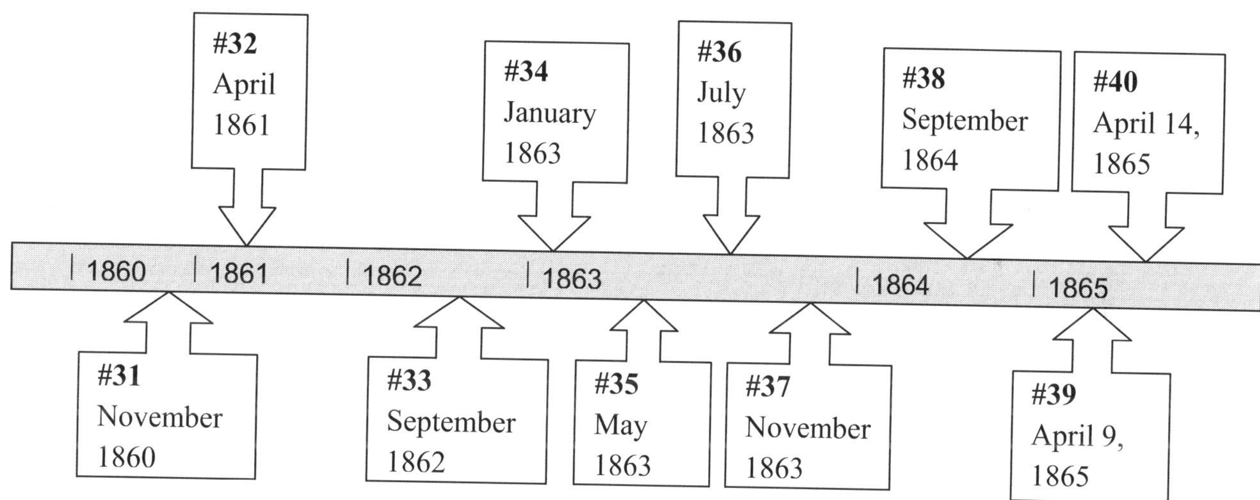

Choices

A. Gettysburg   **B.** Antietam   **C.** Election of 1860   **D.** Gettysburg Address   **E.** Fort Sumter

AB. Emancipation Proclamation   **AC.** Chancellorsville   **AD.** Lincoln's Assassination

AE. End of War   **BC.** Capture of Atlanta

Continue to Next Page

Name ___________________________

Short Answer Questions

1. Explain the events surrounding the secession of the Southern states. (Hint-start with the secession of the first group of states, then explain the secession of the second group of states).

2. Explain the Union war strategy and give examples of how the plan was carried out.

3. Explain how the Emancipation Proclamation affected slavery, why it was issued when it was, and why it did not pertain to all slaves.

4. Explain these passages from the Gettysburg Address:

A) "Four score and seven years ago our fathers brought forth on this continent, a new nation, conceived in Liberty, and dedicated to the proposition that all men are created equal."

B) "But, in a larger sense, we cannot dedicate—we cannot consecrate—we cannot hallow— this ground. The brave men, living and dead, who struggled here, have consecrated it, far about our poor power to add or detract."

5. Explain how the capture of Atlanta helped Lincoln win re-election in November 1864.

Reconstruction (1865-1877)

Official name given to the period of time after the Civil War that referred to the goals of reuniting and rebuilding the country

Major issues of Reconstruction:
Would the South be punished or forgiven?
What would happen to the ex-slaves?
Who would be in charge of Reconstruction?

Two Major plans evolved- Presidential Reconstruction and Congressional (Radical Reconstruction)

Presidential Reconstruction

-Originally Lincoln's plan and followed somewhat by Andrew Johnson after assassination

-Restoring and rebuilding the country was more important than punishing the South

-Believed the South never left Union and offered **amnesty** to those who swore **allegiance**

-Established Freedmen's Bureau in March 1865 to assist ex-slaves

-Restoration of Union should be quick

-Only required 10% of Southern voters to swear oath of loyalty before state could start process of setting up a new government-**10% Plan**

-New southern governments must ratify 13th Amendment

- Johnson pardoned all rebels except former Confederate officeholders and the richest planters.

-Johnson only required southern states to nullify acts of secession, abolish slavery, and refused to pay Confederate government debts

-Johnson's lenient requirements angered many people in Congress and made it possible for many former Confederate leaders to hold political office again

Congressional Reconstruction

-Led by radicals in Congress who really wanted to punish the South

-Believed southern states left Union and forfeited their political rights

-Opposed Presidential Reconstruction especially against Andrew Johnson

-Required majority of voters in South to take oath to Union

-Passed the 14th and 15th Amendments to help ex-slaves in the South (response to Black Codes passed by southern governments)

-Created Five Military districts in the South that oversaw Reconstruction policies and readmission of states

-Impeached Andrew Johnson for interfering with Radical Reconstruction but cited he violated the Tenure of Office Act when he fired Secretary of War

-Created huge resentment by Southerners toward northerners

Reconstruction was neglected with problems during the Grant Presidency (lots of corruption)

Reconstruction officially ended with the **Compromise of 1877**

-Disputed presidential election of 1876 over electoral votes between Democrat, Tilden and Republican, Hayes had to be settled

-It was decided the Republican, Hayes, would get the disputed votes and win the election but must agree to withdraw the military, which was overseeing Reconstruction in the South.

-Remember!! The Democrats were the party of the South and hated the terms of Radical Reconstruction!!

Reconstruction did some good but fell far short of its goals

-Ex-slaves mostly remained poor farmers under the sharecropping and crop-lien systems

-Poll taxes and literacy tests were created to keep blacks from voting

-Jim Crow laws segregated blacks and whites (segregation was upheld by the 1896 Supreme Court case of **Plessy v. Ferguson,** which established the doctrine of **"separate but equal."** Was not overturned until 1954 in Brown v. Topeka)

-The Ku Klux Klan was formed to terrorize blacks and maintain racial supremacy

Study Questions for Reconstruction

1. What does amnesty mean?

2. Whose plan offered amnesty to southerners?

3. How many people in each southern state did Lincoln want to take an oath of loyalty?

4. How many people in each southern state did Congress want to take an oath of loyalty?

5. What organization did the federal government start to help former slaves?

6. Why was President Johnson impeached?

7. Name two main differences between the goals of Lincoln's plan for Reconstruction and Congress' plan for Reconstruction.

8. What was the Compromise of 1877?

9. How did the Compromise of 1877 end Reconstruction?

10. What were black codes?

11. Name the three amendments that were passed during Reconstruction and explain them.

12. What was the Ku Klux Klan?

13. What were Jim Crow laws?

14. Explain the sharecropping and crop-lien systems.

15. What was the major problem during President Grant's administration?

THE SECOND INDUSTRIAL REVOLUTION, THE GROWTH OF CITIES, AND THE PROGRESSIVE MOVEMENT

The following pages contain information and activities for 2nd Industrial Revolution, the growth of urban America, and the Progressive Movement. Since the transformation from a mostly rural to a mainly urban society and the Progressive Movement were by-products of industrialization, the three topics should be taught together in one unit as casual chain of events. The study guide includes many of the important people, events, and concepts students should know. The study guide questions can either be assigned to students to complete over the course of the unit and collected for a grade before the unit exam or the questions can simply serve as self-review study questions. The lecture notes are meant to provide a foundation for information about industrialization and capitalism. The Populist and Grange movements should be covered in more detail by the teacher than is represented in this section. Since students often confuse the Populist Movement and the Progressive Movement it should be emphasized to the students that the Populist Movement was a rural movement whereas the Progressive Movement was an urban movement.

Name______________________________

Study Guide
Industrial Revolution, Growth of Cities, Progressive Movement

Important Terms

Gilded Age
Capitalism
Industrialization
Laissez-faire
Social Darwinism
Gospel of Wealth
Wealth of Nations
Monopoly
Trust
Corporation
Wall Street
Robber Barons

Yellow Dog Contract
Black Lists
Strikes & Lockouts
Labor Unions (KOL)
Collective Bargaining
Haymarket Riot
Pullman Strike
Thomas Edison
Henry Ford
Andrew Carnegie
John Rockefeller
Jay Gould

Cornelius Vanderbilt
J. P. Morgan
Horatio Alger
George Pullman
Samuel Gompers
Frederick Taylor
Vertical Integration
Atlantic Cable
Alexander Bell
Wright Brothers
Cyrus McCormick
Sherman Antitrust

New Immigrants
Assimilation
Nativism
Chinese Exclusion Act
Tenements
Jane Addams
Settlement houses
Social Gospel
Compulsory Education Laws
Conspicuous Consumption
William Randolph Hurst
Yellow Journalism

Progressive Movement Terms

Political Machines
Tammany Hall
Boss Tweed
Gilded Age
Populism
William J. Bryan
"Cross of Gold"

Progressivism
John Dewey
Muckrakers
Lincoln Steffens
Ida Tarbell
Florence Kelley
Muller v. Oregon

Closed Shop
Socialism
I.W.W. (Wobblies)
Daniel Burnham
Prohibition
Booker Washington
W.E.B. Du Bois

Secret Ballot
17th Amendment
Robert La Follette
Theodore Roosevelt
Square Deal
The Jungle
"Bully Pulpit"

William Howard Taft
Graduated Income Tax
Bull Moose Party
Woodrow Wilson
New Freedom
Clayton Antitrust Act
19th Amendment

Critical Thinking Questions

1. Were did much of the wealth and resources that drove the Industrial Revolution come from?
2. What does the term "Gilded Age" mean and why was it applied to this part of American History?
3. Explain the main characteristics of an industrial society.
4. Explain the main characteristics of a capitalistic society. How did those characteristics affect the Industrial Revolution?
5. What were the positive and negative aspects of industrialization?
6. What major inventions and innovations made the Industrial Revolution possible?
7. Explain the contributions Alexander Bell, Henry Ford, Eli Whitney, Robert Fulton, Adam Smith, and Thomas Edison made to the Industrial Revolution.
8. Explain the importance/applications of the steam engine, interchangeable parts, and division of labor.
9. How did the Atlantic Cable, telegraph, telephone, and railroad affect industrialization and society?
10. How did industrialization affect immigration, women, children, and minorities?
11. How did industrialization affect urban growth and the workplace?

12. Who were the Robber Barons? Why were they called this and what did they do?
13. What steps did the government take to encourage industrialization?
14. Explain the Haymarket Riot and Pullman Strike?
15. How was Pullman a "company town?"
16. Explain the weapons of management including the injunction.
17. Explain the weapons of labor.
18. What were the goals of labor unions and how did they conflict with management? Name two labor unions.
19. Explain social Darwinism? Do you agree with it?
20. Explain Andrew Carnegie's "Gospel of Wealth."
21. Explain monopoly, vertical integration, and horizontal integration. Gives some historical and contemporary examples.
22. How did the new immigrants differ from the old immigrants?
23. Give three examples of nativism.
24. Explain the various ways people in the cities relaxed and entertained themselves during this era.
25. What goals did the socialists and Wobblies have in common? How did their views differ on achieving their goals.
26. Explain assimilation and how it was applied during this period in time regarding the new immigrants.
27. What was the Populist Movement and how did it lay the foundation for the Progressive Movement?
28. What was the main difference between the Populist and Progressive movements?
29. Name some progressive leaders and their contributions. Name the three progressive presidents.
30. Explain the opposing views Booker T. Washington and W.E.B. Du Bois had regarding the achievement of equality for black people.
31. Explain how Upton Sinclair's book led to the Meat Inspection Act and the Pure Food and Drug Act.
32. Explain how Teddy Roosevelt was the conservation president.
33. Explain the 16th Amendment and the concept of a graduated income tax.
34. What event led to President Taft losing the support of Teddy Roosevelt and other progressives?
35. How did Teddy Roosevelt's idea of trust-busting differ from Woodrow Wilson's?
36. How did Wilson's support of the Federal Reserve Act seem to contradict his belief in small business yet also support the progressive idea of more governmental control?
37. What event brought about the end of the Progressive Movement?

Second Industrial Revolution

Refers to the period when goods began to be mass produced by machines

Driving force behind industrialization was capitalism

-ideas put forth in Adam Smith's book *The Wealth of Nations* (1776)

Made possible by new inventions and innovations in technology and production after the Civil War

Also made possible by the disappearance of the old South's anti-northern, anti-commercial practices

Railroads very important to the Industrial Revolution

Much of the wealth and materials (minerals) needed for industrialization came from the West, such as large deposits of gold, silver, iron ore, oil, etc.

Characteristics of the Industrial Revolution

-change from hand production of goods to machine production

-change from home production of goods to factory production

-mass production= more goods faster and cheaper

-industrialization greatly increased immigration to U.S. (this time mostly from southern and eastern Europe)

-large migration of people from rural areas to urban areas, and some cities became large manufacturing and business centers (Chicago).

-change from a mostly agricultural society to a predominantly manufacturing society

Characteristics of capitalism

-private ownership of property and means of production/distribution

-desire for profit and accumulation of wealth

-Laissez-faire capitalism referred to a completely hands-off approach to business and the economy by the government…no regulation

-lack of oversight allowed companies to grow and prosper in the free market

-competition for goods (leads to lower prices, better products, and more choices for consumers)

-law of supply and demand greatly determines prices, wages, rents, etc.

Key inventions and innovations of the Second Industrial Revolution

-steam power now produced mechanical energy and electricity

-Bessemer Process of steel production

-light bulb

-division of labor (idea already existed but fully implemented at this time as with the assembly line)

-interchangeable parts (Eli Whitney formerly used this idea in his manufacturing of guns but now adopted on a wide scale)

-improvements in transportation (railroad) and communication (telegraph and telephone)

-organization of businesses into large corporations that were able to raise huge amounts of money by selling stock

Problems with early industrialization

-people worked for long hours in dangerous factory conditions

-child labor

-monopolies came to control industries and drive out competition

-no laws to protect workers, consumers, or environment

-overcrowding of cities

-contamination of the environment and pollution of cities

-conflict between workers and management led to strikes and riots

-loss of skilled labor jobs to machines resulted in lower pay for many people

-many of these problems would later lead to the Progressive Movement

LESSON PLAN
INDUSTRIAL REVOLUTION EXCEL PROJECT

Teacher:	Date:
Subject:	Period(s):
Title of Lesson:	State Standards:
Common Core Standards and Indicators: **RH.9-10.7.** Integrate quantitative or technical analysis (e.g., charts, research data) with qualitative analysis in print or digital text **RH.11-12.7.** Integrate and evaluate multiple sources of information presented in diverse formats and media (e.g., visually, quantitatively, as well as in words) in order to address a question or solve a problem	College Readiness Standards: **ACT-CR: Reading, ACT-CR: Score Range 16–19 Generalizations and Conclusions:** Draw simple generalizations and conclusions about people, ideas, and so on in uncomplicated passages

Purpose/ Objective	To enhance students' knowledge of the 2nd Industrial Revolution while also teaching them how to use Microsoft Excel.
Materials	Project directions contained on the following page, textbook, Internet, other teacher-supplied resources, LCD projector, computer with Microsoft Excel
Procedures	Divide the students into cooperative groups. Pass out copies of directions for the project. Explain the directions. Display a sample Excel spreadsheet to the class using a computer and LCD projector. Explain how to set up the spreadsheet using the examples given on the second page of the directions. Explain the basic mathematical functions of Excel to students and show them some simple formulas. Students should take notes on how to set up their spreadsheet.
Assessment	Teacher will determine how many points this project is worth and can grade it using a rubric or a sliding scale.
Comments	A working knowledge of Excel is required by the teacher. Examples of how to set up the spreadsheet are included with the directions, but the mathematical formulas are not. Figuring out how to write the formulas in the proper cells will be part of the students' learning curve though the teacher should help them with this by giving them some examples.

Industrial Revolution Excel Project

Microsoft Excel is an extremely powerful and versatile database program used by people all over the world. It has countless types of personal, business, and educational applications. Excel's pages, or spreadsheets, are used to collect, organize, manipulate, and display a variety of information. It is used to keep track of personal information such as names and addresses, which can be used to create letters and mailings. It is used to track business inventory, sort and calculate mathematical data, and keep lists of information that can be imported into other programs. Excel can also use the information in its database to create charts, graphs, and other graphic representations of information to facilitate the further analysis of the data.

The 2nd Industrial Revolution (1865-1905) brought about monumental changes for the United States as new inventions and innovations began the transformation of our country into mainly an urban, manufacturing society and economy. New inventions and the massive increase in the production of goods by machines created new businesses and industries that would need a large labor force to sustain the country's economic growth. This demand for labor was filled by the millions of immigrants from southern and eastern Europe who came to the United States during this period. You are going to use Microsoft Excel to organize and chart information about the millions of "new immigrants" who came to America between 1880 and 1910 to illustrate the correlation between the Industrial Revolution and the resulting population changes in our country.

Resources/Websites:http://www.census.gov/
http://www.census.gov/population/www/censusdata/hiscendata.html

Steps:

1. Go to the U.S. Census Bureau website to research population information between 1880 and 1910. Use the "Selected Historical Decennial Population Counts" for 1790-1990 and 1850-1990 for this assignment.

2. Research the total population growth between 1880 and 1910.

3. Research the number of foreign born people between 1880 and 1910 and research the various countries of origin for many of the new immigrants.

4. Research the population growth of Chicago, New York, Philadelphia, and St. Louis between 1880 and 1910.

5. Research the shift in rural to urban population between 1880 and 1910.

6. Set up your Microsoft Excel categories (columns and rows) using the information you have already collected. Use separate Excel sheets for steps 2-6.

7. Write a mathematical formula to make the program calculate the totals in each of the categories.

8. Use the program to display the results on a chart or graph. Use the graphs and analysis questions to draw conclusions about the Industrial Revolution and the population changes. Be able to explain your conclusions to the class.

Industrial Revolution Excel Project

Sample Excel Spreadsheets

#2, #3, #6

	A	B	C	D	E	F
1		1880	1890	1900	1910	Total
2	U.S. Population					
3	Foreign Born					
4	Rural Population					
5	Urban Population					

#4

	A	B	C	D	E	F
1		1880	1890	1900	1910	Total
2	Italy					
3	Greece					
4	Hungary					
5	Poland					

#5

	A	B	C	D	E	F
1		1880	1890	1900	1910	Total
2	Chicago					
3	New York					
4	Philadelphia					
5	St. Louis					

Analysis Questions

1. What is the correlation between the Industrial Revolution and this second great wave of immigration? What does this tell you about the countries the immigrants were coming from during this period?

2. How did the Industrial Revolution affect the growth of cities? Why did this happen?

3. Where did many of the immigrants settle when they came to the United States?

4. How did the huge influx of immigrants affect various cities and the country as a whole?

LESSON PLAN
PROGRESSIVE MOVEMENT CHART

Teacher:	Date:
Subject:	Period(s):
Title of Lesson:	State Standards:
Common Core Standards and Indicators: **RH.11-12.2.** Determine the central ideas or information of a primary or secondary source; provide an accurate summary that makes clear the relationships among the key details and ideas	College Readiness Standards: **ACT-CR: Reading, ACT-CR: Score Range 20–23** **Sequential, Comparative, and Cause-Effect Relationships**: Identify clear relationships between people, ideas, and so on in uncomplicated passages **ACT-CR: Reading, ACT-CR: Score Range 16–19** **Generalizations and Conclusions:** Draw simple generalizations and conclusions about people, ideas, and so on in uncomplicated passages

Purpose/ Objective	Students will learn more about many of the progressive leaders and the reforms they championed while enhancing their literacy skills by identifying cause and effect relationships, drawing conclusions and generalizations, and making inferences from the text to complete a chart on the Progressive Movement.
Materials	Copies of blank chart contained on the following page, transparency of blank chart, and completed chart (follows blank chart on next page) to be used as an answer key, textbook, Internet
Procedures	Pass out copies of blank charts to students and put transparency of blank chart on overhead. Access students' prior knowledge then explain activity to students. • Students must use the one or two clues given to find the missing information necessary to complete the chart. For example…**John Dewey** was concerned with **education** (those are the two clues given for the second item on the chart). Students should read about John Dewey in their textbook and figure out what solution he or other reformers proposed about education. Teacher should examine completed chart on page 180 for a better understanding of how students should complete the chart. Complete one or two items on the chart with the students as an example. When students have completed the chart use the transparency of the completed chart with key of suggested answers so they can check their work.
Assessment	Grade according to a standard scale.
Comments	This is a time-consuming and difficult assignment for many students. It is not meant to be easy so be patient. Allow students to work on activity in class for a couple days so teacher can assist them.

Progressive Movement

Problem/Event	Solution	Person/People
Workplace		
Education		
		John Dewey
		Jane Addams
		Muckrakers
		Lincoln Steffens
	McClure's Magazine	
Standard Oil trust		Ida Tarbell
	Sister Carrie	
	Democracy & Social Ethics	
Child labor	National Child Labor Committee	
Triangle Shirtwaist Fire		
	Muller v. Oregon	
	Closed shop	
Workers' Rights		Samuel Gompers
Tenement housing		
		Daniel Burnham
Moral Reform		
		W. E. B. Du Bois
	NAACP	
Assimilation of Immigrants		
	17th Amendment	
	Initiative, Referendum, Recall	
		Robert La Follette
	Square Deal	Theodore Roosevelt
Trust-busting		
	The Jungle	Upton Sinclair
	Meat Inspection Act/Pure Food and Drug Act	
	Protecting the Environment	
		William Howard Taft
	Bull Moose Party	
	New Freedom	Woodrow Wilson
	Clayton Antitrust Act	Woodrow Wilson
	Socialism	Eugene Debs
Women's Suffrage		Elizabeth Cady Stanton/Susan B. Anthony

Definition of "progressivism":

Definition of "bully pulpit":

Definition of "Square Deal":

Definition of "New Freedom":

Progressive Movement

Problem/Event	Solution	Person/People
Workplace	8-hour day/minimum wage	Progressive leaders/lawmakers&unions
Education	real-life activities	John Dewey
Social Reform	Settlement houses/Hull House	Jane Addams
Corruption/Greed	Expose them in press	Muckrakers
Corruption/Greed	*Tweed Days in St. Louis*	Lincoln Steffens
Corruption/Greed	McClure's Magazine	Various writers
Standard Oil trust	*History of the Standard Oil Company*	Ida Tarbell
Greedy Business	*Sister Carrie*	*Theodore Dreiser*
Social Responsibility	*Democracy & Social Ethics*	Jane Addams
Child Labor	National Child Labor Committee	Florence Kelley
Triangle Shirtwaist Fire	Fire safety codes	Rose Schneiderman
Challenge ten-hour day	*Muller v. Oregon*	*Louis Brandeis*
Workers' Rights	Closed shop	Unions
Workers' Rights	American Federation of Labor	Samuel Gompers
Tenement Housing	Tenement House Act	Lawrence Veiller
Dirty Cities	City Planning	Daniel Burnham
Moral Reform	Prohibition	Billy Sunday/Congress
Discrimination	Racial Equality	W. E. B. Du Bois
Discrimination	NAACP	W. E. B. Du Bois
Assimilation of Immigrants	Public Schools	William Maxwell
Election Reform	17th Amendment	Congress
Election Reform	Initiative, Referendum, Recall	State Progressives
Public Interest	Wisconsin Idea	Robert La Follette
Balance Business & Labor	Square Deal	Theodore Roosevelt
Trust-busting	44 Law Suits v. businesses	Theodore Roosevelt
Protecting Consumer	*The Jungle*	Upton Sinclair
Protecting Consumer	Meat Inspection Act/Pure Food and Drug Act	Theodore Roosevelt
Protecting the Environment	Conservation/Reclamation	Theodore Roosevelt/Gifford Pinchot
Graduated Income Tax	16th Amendment	William Howard Taft
Continue Reforms	Bull Moose Party	Theodore Roosevelt
Support Small Business	New Freedom	Woodrow Wilson
Limit Monopolies	Clayton Antitrust Act	Woodrow Wilson
Workers' Rights	Socialism (public ownership of industry)	Eugene Debs
Women's Suffrage	19th Amendment	Elizabeth C. Stanton/Susan B. Anthony

Definition of "progressivism": Urban movement aimed at solving many of the problems created by the 2nd Industrial Revolution

Definition of "bully pulpit": Theodore Roosevelt's belief to use the presidency to speak out about important issues

Definition of "Square Deal": Theodore Roosevelt's promise to balance the interests of workers, consumers, and business

Definition of "New Freedom": President Wilson's plan to encourage more small business

LESSON PLAN
INDUSTRIAL REVOLUTION WEB DIAGRAM AND SUMMARY

Teacher:	Date:
Subject:	Period(s):
Title of Lesson:	State Standards:
Common Core Standards and Indicators: **RH.11-12.2.** Determine the central ideas or information of a primary or secondary source; provide an accurate summary that makes clear the relationships among the key details and ideas	College Readiness Standards: **ACT-CR: Reading, ACT-CR: Score Range 24–27 Main Ideas and Author's Approach:** Summarize basic events and ideas in more challenging passages

Purpose/ Objective	To help students understand, review, and summarize some of the important aspects of the 2nd Industrial Revolution.
Materials	White board and markers or chalkboard, student notes and assignments on related topics
Procedures	Teacher will lead the class in a review of important aspects of the Industrial Revolution. Students will guide the teacher in completing the web diagram. Draw a circle in the center of the board and in the circle write "2nd Industrial Revolution." Ask students to recall some of the important events they have recently learned about the Industrial Revolution. Important events should be organized in other circles as main ideas in the creation of a web diagram that further explains the main topic. Use the diagram on the next page as a guide. Ask students to recall specific supporting details about each main idea and write them next to the circles, like spokes coming off the hub of a bicycle tire.
Assessment	Ask students to write a summary of the events using the web diagram as a guide. Tell students they should simply use the main ideas and supporting details in the diagram to reconstruct the information in paragraph form.
Comments	This same technique of using a web diagram to explain and summarize events and concepts can be beneficial to students with low reading abilities as well as special education students, both of whom often benefit from more graphic representations of information.

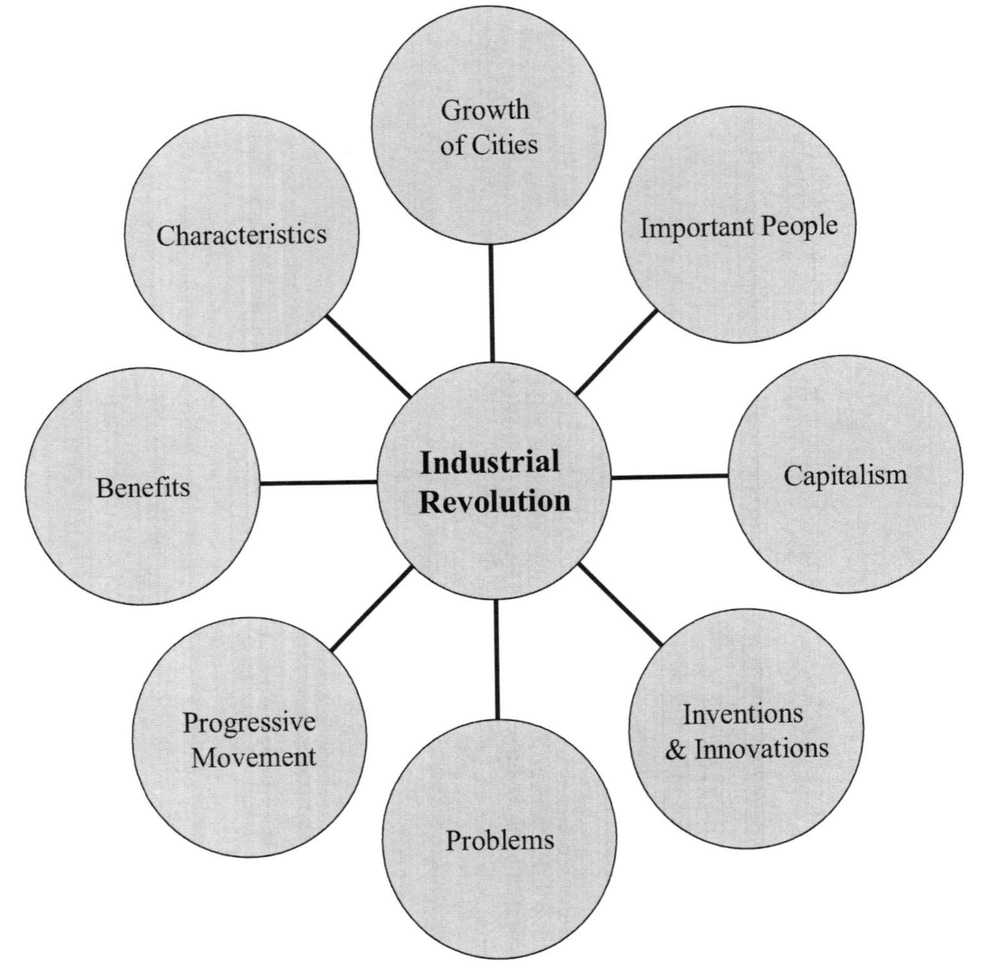
Industrial Revolution
Growth of Cities
Important People
Capitalism
Inventions & Innovations
Problems
Progressive Movement
Benefits
Characteristics

LESSON PLAN
PROGRESSIVE MOVEMENT NEWSPAPER PROJECT

Teacher:	Date:
Subject:	Period(s):
Title of Lesson:	State Standards:
Common Core Standards and Indicators: **RH.11-12.2.** Determine the central ideas or information of a primary or secondary source; provide an accurate summary that makes clear the relationships among the key details and ideas **WHST.11-12.2a.** Introduce a topic and organize complex ideas, concepts, and information so that each new element builds on that which precedes it to create a unified whole; include formatting (e.g., headings), graphics (e.g., figures, tables), and multimedia when useful to aiding comprehension.	College Readiness Standards: **ACT-CR: Reading, ACT-CR: Score Range 16–19 Generalizations and Conclusions:** Draw simple generalizations and conclusions about people, ideas, and so on in uncomplicated passages

Purpose/ Objective	Students will display their knowledge of the problems caused by the 2nd Industrial Revolution and the resulting reforms initiated during the Progressive Movement by creating a fictitious newspaper, brochure, or newsletter that explains some of the accomplishments of the Progressive Movement to the people living at that time.
Materials	Project directions contained on following page and grading rubric; textbook; Internet; other materials and activities related to 2nd Industrial Revolution, urbanization, and the Progressive Movement; Microsoft Publisher or similar software
Procedures	Divide class in cooperative learning groups if desired. Distribute project directions. Allow students class time to work on project and time in computer lab. Completed projects should be printed by groups and shared with the class.
Assessment	Project can be graded using the sample project grading scale included with this assignment or teacher can create their own rubric.
Comments	Students can email completed project to teacher for grading or teacher can grade the printed version submitted by students.

Progressive Movement Project

The Industrial Revolution brought about many positive changes in our country. However, the changes came with many negative consequences that had to be addressed. Many of the problems created by the Industrial Revolution led to the Progressive Movement, which was a period of reform and improvement in the daily lives of people. All types of problems from urban pollution, poverty, political corruption, unfair business practices, the regulation of the food industry, to the protection of the environment were addressed by progressive leaders. Many famous politicians such as Theodore Roosevelt and Woodrow Wilson led the fight to improve the quality of life for many people in our country during this time.

Your assignment is to create a newspaper, brochure, or newsletter that outlines the major problems progressive leaders wanted to solve as well as the methods they used to achieve their goals. Your newsletter should be written from the point of view of a progressive leader or newspaper reporter of the time living in a major city during the early 1900s. This newsletter should clearly explain and illustrate the major social, economic, political, and environmental problems of the time and what has been done to address these problems. Therefore, your newsletter should attempt to influence the public about the need for change and the need to support progressive leaders. Your newsletter should include simple-to-read text as well as pictures, cartoons, or any images that illustrate the goals and people of the Progressive Movement. Your project should be done with Microsoft Publisher. Your grading scale is on the back.

Progressive Movement Project

The Industrial Revolution brought about many positive changes in our country. However, the changes came with many negative consequences that had to be addressed. Many of the problems created by the Industrial Revolution led to the Progressive Movement, which was a period of reform and improvement in the daily lives of people. All types of problems from urban pollution, poverty, political corruption, unfair business practices, the regulation of the food industry, to the protection of the environment were addressed by progressive leaders. Many famous politicians such as Theodore Roosevelt and Woodrow Wilson led the fight to improve the quality of life for many people in our country during this time.

Your assignment is to create a newspaper, brochure, or newsletter that outlines the major problems progressive leaders wanted to solve as well as the methods they used to achieve their goals. Your newsletter should be written from the point of view of a progressive leader or newspaper reporter of the time living in a major city during the early 1900s. This newsletter should clearly explain and illustrate the major social, economic, political, and environmental problems of the time and what has been done to address these problems. Therefore, your newsletter should attempt to influence the public about the need for change and the need to support progressive leaders. Your newsletter should include simple-to-read text as well as pictures, cartoons, or any images that illustrate the goals and people of the Progressive Movement. Your project should be done with Microsoft Publisher. Your grading scale is on the back.

Progressive Movement Project Rubric

Name______________________________ Period__________ Date_________________

Grading Rubric

Accuracy of information (20pts.) __________

Creativity (20pts.) __________

Included all required information (20pts.) __________

Effort and followed all directions (20pts.) __________

Overall effectiveness of presentation (20pts.) __________

Total points =100

Your score __________

Comments:

____

____

____

____

Progressive Movement Project Rubric

Name______________________________ Period__________ Date_________________

Grading Rubric

Accuracy of information (20pts.) __________

Creativity (20pts.) __________

Included all required information (20pts.) __________

Effort and followed all directions (20pts.) __________

Overall effectiveness of presentation (20pts.) __________

Total points =100

Your score __________

Comments:

____

____

____

____

Industrialization and Urbanization Test

1. All of the following are characteristics of capitalism Except:
   a) private ownership b) competition c) profit d) high level of government control

2. All of the following are characteristics of industrialization Except:
   a) mass production b) use of machines c) less urbanization d) growth of cities

3. The government's policy toward business during the era of industrialization could best be described as
   a) more regulation b) Laissez-faire c) high tax rates d. low tax rates

4. A monopoly exists when:
   a) there is no competition b) prices are fixed c) one company controls an industry d) all of the above

5. Monopolies are good for the consumer.
   a) True b) False

6. All of the following had a role in the Industrial Revolution Except:
   a) interchangeable parts b) division of labor c) steam power d) solar power

7. A company that has many investors is called a:
   a) trust b) corporation c) sole proprietorship d) limited partnership

8. Which was not a characteristic of the Industrial Revolution?

   a) shift from rural to urban living

   b) shift from hand production to machine production of goods

   c) shift from an agricultural to a manufacturing society

   d) shift from factory work to home-based businesses

9. Which book did Adam Smith write that outlined the principles of capitalism?
   a) Gospel of Wealth b) Money Talks c) social Darwinism d) Wealth of Nations

10. What name did Mark Twain give the era of the Industrialization Revolution?
    a) Gilded Age b) Age of Wealth c) Age of Industry d) Social Gospel

11. What was Mark Twain referring to when he gave the era of industrialization its other name?
    a) lack of regulation b) corruption and greed c) unsafe working conditions d) enormous wealth

12. Who was not a captain of industry?
    a) Rockefeller b) Carnegie c) J.P. Morgan d) Samuel Gompers

13. Who was not a robber baron?
    a) Rockefeller b) Carnegie c) J.P. Morgan d) Samuel Gompers

14. Who invented the telephone?
    a) Edison b) Bell c) Ford d) Wright Brothers

15. Who invented the light bulb?
    a) Edison b) Bell c) Ford d) Wright Brothers

16. Mass production causes the price of products to go down.
    a) True b) False

17. Who invented the airplane?
    a) Edison b) Bell c) Ford d) Wright Brothers

18. Who was known for his work with labor unions?
    a) Rockefeller b) Carnegie c) J.P. Morgan d) Samuel Gompers

19. Which was not a labor union?
    a) Knights of Labor b) American Federation of Labor c) both d) neither

20. Which methods were used by management to control workers?
    a) yellow dog contracts b) blacklists c) lockouts d) all of the above

21. Which of the following were used by workers to get what they wanted?
    a) strikes b) collective bargaining c) both d) neither

22. Who invented the telegraph?
    a) Morse b) Bell c) Edison d) Fulton

23. What Chicago man built railroad cars?
    a) George Pullman b) George Jefferson c) Richard Sears d) Montgomery Ward

24. What concept justified the huge amounts of money some people were making?
a) Gospel of Wealth b) Money Talks c) social Darwinism d) Wealth of Nations

25. What famous event took place in Chicago over labor unrest?
a) Pullman strike b) Haymarket riot c) both d) neither

26. Where did the "new immigrants" mainly come from during the Industrial Revolution?
a) northern & western Europe b) southern & eastern Europe c) China d) Mexico

27. What term refers to fitting into a new society or becoming like everyone else?
a) nativism b) assimilation c) Darwinism d) socialism

28. What term refers to favoring American-born people over foreign-born people?
a) nativism b) assimilation c) Darwinism d) socialism

29. All of the following would be considered progressive people Except:
a) Jane Addams b) John Dewey c) Florence Kelly d) Henry Ford

30. All of the following were progressive presidents Except:
a) T. Roosevelt b) Grant c) Taft d) Wilson

31. The group of journalists who exposed many of the problems during the Industrial Revolution were:
a) socialists b) Wobblies c) populists d) muckrakers

32. Who was concerned with urban poverty?
a) John Dewey b) Upton Sinclair c) Ida Tarbell d) Jane Addams

33. Who was concerned with education?
a) John Dewey b) Upton Sinclair c) Ida Tarbell d) Jane Addams

34. What book was written about the problems in the meat packing industry?
a) The Jungle b) Gospel of Wealth c) Wealth of Nations d) Social Gospel

35. Which progressive president was most concerned with the environment?
a) T. Roosevelt b) Grant c) Taft d) Wilson

36. Which progressive president ran under the Bull Moose Party?
a) T. Roosevelt b) Grant c) Taft d) Wilson

37. Progressivism was mainly an urban movement?
    a) True b) False

38. What event brought new immigrants to the United States in the late 1800s and early 1900s?
    a) Civil War b) Industrial Revolution c) WWI d) Agricultural Revolution

39. All of the following were progressive reforms Except:
    a) 18th Amendment b) 19th Amendment c) end to child labor d) end to large companies

40. All of the following are explanations of the Progressive Movement Except:
    a) attempt to reform corruption in government

    b) attempt to solve social and economic problems in the cities

    c) attempt to reform business practices

    d) attempt to reform manufacturing methods

41. Which amendment concerned women's suffrage?
    a) 16th b) 17th c) 18th d) 19th

42. Which amendment concerned the prohibition of alcohol?
    a) 16th b) 17th c) 18th d) 19th

43. All of the following are economic systems Except:
    a) capitalism b) communism c) socialism d) Darwinism

44. The Chinese Exclusion Act was an example of:
    a) nativism b) assimilation c) Darwinism d) socialism

45. What event led to the end of the Progressive Movement?
    a) Civil War b) Industrial Revolution c) WWI d) Agricultural Revolution

Answer the following questions on a separate sheet of paper.

1. Define Industrial Revolution.
2. Define social Darwinism.
3. Explain how the "old immigrants" differed from the "new immigrants."
4. Define progressivism.
5. Explain the difference between capitalism and communism.

Made in the USA
Middletown, DE
05 November 2015